IT'S NOT THE BIG
THAT EAT THE SMALL...
IT'S THE FAST
THAT EAT THE SLOW

IT'S NOT THE BIG
THAT EAT THE SMALL ...
IT'S THE FAST
THAT EAT THE SLOW

➡ ➡ ➡

HOW TO USE SPEED AS A
COMPETITIVE TOOL IN BUSINESS

JASON JENNINGS

AND

LAURENCE HAUGHTON

HarperBusiness
An Imprint of HarperCollins*Publishers*

This book is dedicated to everyone who understands the difference between management and leadership.

HarperCollins books may be purchased for educational, business, or sales promotional use. For information please write: Special Markets Department, HarperCollins Publishers Inc., 10 East 53rd Street, New York, NY 10022.

First HarperBusiness paperback edition published 2002

Designed by Jackie McKee

The Library of Congress has catalogued the hardcover edition as follows:
Jennings, Jason.
    It's not the big that eat the small . . . it's the fast that eat the slow:
how to use speed as a competitive tool in business / by Jason Jennings
& Laurence Haughton.—1st ed.
        p. cm.
    Includes index.
    ISBN 0-06-662053-8 (alk. paper)
    1. Strategic planning. 2. Competition. 3. Time—Economic aspects.
4. Creative ability in business. I. Haughton, Laurence. II. Title.
HD30.28 .J46 2001
658.4—dc21   00-047l93

ISBN 0-06-662054-6 (pbk.)

02 03 04 05 06 RRD 10 9 8 7 6 5 4 3 2 1

We few, we happy few, we band of brothers;
For he today that sheds his blood with me
Shall be my brother; be he ne 're so vile
This day shall gentle his condition;
And gentlemen in England, now abed,
Shall think themselves accursed they were not here;
And hold their manhoods cheap whiles any speaks
That fought with us upon Saint Crispin's day.

—William Shakespeare

Henry V, act 4, scene 3

THANKS . . . AND . . .

We want to gratefully acknowledge the invaluable assistance of the people who helped us in researching and writing this book.

First and foremost our clients around the world must be thanked. For the past two decades they've allowed us to report our findings and observations and have served as our laboratory. In the process, they led us to discoveries and knowledge that we were able to transmit to others. There is nothing we enjoy more than teaching, helping, learning from, and being with our *customers*.

Special thanks to Bruce Ritter, an investment counselor in San Rafael, California, who specializes in advising and managing the investments of high net worth individuals and families. During our research and writing, he answered hundreds of our urgent telephone calls and queries. Whenever we needed information fast about a company's financial performance or help with gaining access, he responded with accurate answers and opened doors.

Our thanks and respect go to Tenney Campbell, one of the best businessmen on the planet. He is most rare among business executives: an individual who is able to combine the wisdom gained from nearly a half century in the school of hard knocks with the intellectual firepower of the best "B" school academician. His suggested readings and straight-talk critiques helped shape this book.

Adrian Zackheim, a vice president of HarperCollins, provided us the opportunity of moving from consulting, speaking, hosting, and teaching into authorship. His bet on us won't be forgotten.

It's awful to lose an editor who has become your friend midway through such a major project, but before he left Harper Collins Zach Schisgal made certain we were on track and helped us develop the blueprint for condensing a voluminous amount of research into what is, hopefully, a carefully thought out and well-organized work.

We knew we were near the finish line when our new editor, Edwin Tan, spent a torturous all-night fourteen-hour flight from New York to Singapore squished between crying babies reading the finished manuscript from first page to last and, upon arrival, declared the manuscript a success. Every change he suggested was right on target and Edwin became the book's leading cheerleader. We owe him and hope to work with him again soon.

We also need to thank our respective families. Alongside busy consulting, teaching, and speaking schedules, this project consumed every available emotional and physical moment. Special thanks to George, Nancy, Nick, and Robbie for their understanding.

As we neared the completion of our research, we developed a hypothesis, namely, that the tactics practiced by the world's fastest companies could serve as a predictive indicator of a company's future financial performance. Believing that all the companies profiled in this book have real staying power, we've *put our money where our pens are* and made an equity investment in each and are constantly searching for start-ups who practice the tactics explained in this book.

Gaining access to the leaders profiled in these pages (with the exception of Clear Channel Communications, Charles Schwab, and Lend Lease) wasn't easy. In most instances gatekeepers, in a misguided demonstration of their own pompous sense of self-importance and value, did their best to prevent *any* contact with or access to the brass.

But we persevered and ultimately prevailed. Once inside, we found every business leader to be fascinating, revealing, humble, keenly interested, and interesting. They were gracious and provided us unprecedented access to the tactics and strategies they've used to distinguish themselves as the fastest businesses on the planet. This book wouldn't have been possible without their help.

But while we sincerely thank them, we can't help pass along an observation: The morgues are full of business executives with a tag on their toe, who, upon achieving great success, came to rely exclusively on the eyes, ears, and views of their self-serving minions, who counseled, "You're far too important to deal with people. We'll take care of that for you." Or who, on their own, came to believe, "I'm too busy now to deal with customers," and . . . in so doing isolated themselves from the outside world. Failure inevitably followed.

Will the leaders of the fastest companies in the world maintain their edge by staying close and accessible to the marketplace? We hope so.

CONTENTS

INTRODUCTION TO THE PAPERBACK EDITION

WHY A BOOK ON SPEED?

You've got every right to wonder: Just what planet are you guys from?

After all, you're already working incredibly hard, getting more done with less . . . and here we are with a book saying you've still got to get a lot faster.

We'd like to tell you it's not our fault . . . but that wouldn't be accurate. Almost ten years ago we created the phrase, "It's not the big that eat the small . . . It's the fast that eat the slow" to make it clear that quick thinking and fast action had replaced size as a competitive advantage. It simply was time that we addressed the question, how can business get faster? And before we go any further, let us respond to that "what planet" crack above with a preview of a big discovery you'll find inside: Being fast has less to do with working longer or harder than with the things you stop doing and how you remove *speed bumps!*

Our research into companies and business situations where speed was critical took two paths.

One of us looked at financial comparisons to find some of the recent winners in the eat-or-be-eaten arena. Among others we got the stories of:

AOL who in 1995 was bleeding cash and getting razzed by Silicon Valley and in the next five years swallowed Netscape, then Time Warner and has proved all the tech pundits wrong.

Clear Channel Communications, labeled "just a tire kicker from San Antonio" by media experts in the 1980s and now spanning the globe as the world's largest out-of-home media operator.

Charles Schwab who started at a folding table with the feeling that Wall Street had it all wrong and quickly became the dominant name in discount and on-line financial services.

The other one looked at the psychological, philosophical, and practical challenges to making speed a competitive advantage in organizations:

What is the difference *between speed and haste* and what can business do to end any confusion?

How can a business *look at the world with new eyes* and get the fresh perspectives that will keep it ahead of the competition?

How can leaders help their people to stop dreading high
velocity and rediscover *the thrill of deciding, acting, and
staying fast*?

Together we share 26 strategies and tactics for making speed a competitive tool for you. And in keeping with the theme, we ruthlessly
edited this book to make it a fast read with lots of take-away value.

But since the hardcover edition came out, we have thought
more about the reasons for embracing speed. We've come to
believe speed is not something you have to "hold your nose" to
master . . . the new faster business environment is no bitter pill to
swallow or even a two-edged sword.

Speed will bring changes that can make the business world
better for everyone.

OUR FIRST BIG LESSON
IN SPEED—ABANDONMENT!

Originally, we wanted to write another book, one that revealed
the seven guiding principles we'd found, during our twenty years
of consulting and teaching, to be common to the most successful
companies in the world. But our publisher didn't like that idea,
and eventually, eager to be published by a major publishing
house, we gave it up and worked feverishly to create a book they
liked.

Our need to abandon turned out to be a fitting metaphor for
the book. As we discovered, you can't be truly fast until you master the art of letting go and abandoning those things that are making or keeping you slow.

While the original manuscript doesn't deal in depth with the issue of abandonment, upon reflection, we could have spent a lot more time on the subject. As we travel the world consulting and speaking, we've discovered that most people believe their companies' inability to abandon egos and old breadwinners, and those companies' collective need to defend earlier choices significantly slow them down and hinder their ability to be fast. We hope a future book will deal with how to institutionalize abandonment.

Charles Schwab, who launched his firm with four stockbrokers sitting around a table trading shares, had to abandon his belief that salespeople couldn't give advice, which for many years was a firing offense at Schwab, and still be ethical. Within two years of abandoning that belief, advice made up 40 percent of the firm's profits and Schwab had a greater than 30 percent market share of all stock trades executed in the U.S.

Andy Grove of Intel was on record as saying that his company would never manufacture a chip for the sub-$1,000 PC market, referring to it as Segment Zero. Earlier in life he'd abandoned his hopes of being an opera singer when it was pointed out he couldn't sing, and later he had to abandon his dream of being a journalist when he was told he couldn't write. His demonstrated ability to abandon served him well when he was able to let go of his distaste for a segment of the marketplace, turn his company upside down, and lead the effort to create Celeron, the most successful chip in his firm's history.

When you refuse to abandon, bad things always seem to happen. Steve Jobs couldn't abandon an antiquated distribution system and eventually got his clock cleaned by Michael Dell, who dared to question why you needed distributors to sell computers. Jobs couldn't let go of his ego, reasoning, we guess, that if you're a visionary you must always be right.

GE Capital kept pouring good money after bad into their refinances of Montgomery Wards when everyone's grandfather knew the concept was dead and had been calling it "Monkey Wards" for years. Was granddad prescient or just unburdened by the need to defend his earlier decisions?

Consider the shareholder money wasted by General Motors as they revved up the budget for one final time in a last-gasp effort to convince the public, "It's not your father's Oldsmobile," while the whole world laughed knowing it was great-grandpa's Oldsmobile. GM couldn't abandon yesterday's breadwinner.

FOUR REASONS WHY WE LOVE SPEED (AND WHY YOU SHOULD TOO)

#1   An Instant Message for Slow CEOs: Don't Let the Door Hit You in the Ass on Your Way Out

The first reason we love speed: It is revolutionizing the terms of tenure for executives everywhere. Years ago anyone who made it to the executive suite could set his sights on a good long run. But not anymore.

In the eight months through February 2001, the rate at which CEOs were replaced was up almost 40 percent. (The next levels of management have churned even faster.) This is not a matter of bosses finding greener pastures; Rakesh Khurana of MIT has found that chief executives hired since 1985 are three times as likely to be fired.

We believe this new shortened "life expectancy" at headquarters has the potential for enormous payback. The story of physicist Max Planck illustrates why: In 1918, Planck was awarded the Nobel Prize "in recognition of epoch-making investigations" in physics. "Epoch-making" is a huge accolade. It means Planck's ideas advanced the science and brought about a whole new era.

But forty-four years earlier the establishment scolded Max for questioning the science of physics: At the age of 16, Max Planck met with Philipp Von Jolly, his professor of physics at the University of Munich. Von Jolly told him that physics was essentially a "complete science" with "little prospect of further developments." You can almost hear his admonition "My dear Master Planck . . . let's not waste your time and mine trying to reinvent the wheel."

That experience had to have influenced Max Planck as he created his famous dictum. He recounts in *The Philosophy of Physics*:

> An important scientific innovation rarely makes its way by gradually winning over and converting its opponents. . . . What happens is that its opponents gradually die out and that the next generation is familiarized with the ideas from the beginning.

It's not just in science that a closed-minded hierarchy stifles innovation and promotes inertia. Bill Bowerman, who with his student Phil Knight and his wife's waffle iron revolutionized the sneaker industry, was originally told to stick to coaching and stop telling the footwear bosses how to create athletic shoes. In 1986, Philippe Kahn of Borland said, "All this bull about Windows . . . none of it is useful . . .

and none of it will change the way people work." (Even young Bill Gates once thought "640k ought to be enough for anybody.")

What have you heard in your career?

"We can't be distracted by new initiatives. The leading edge is the bleeding edge." (In other words, leave the innovation to others. We'll play catch-up.)

"Our distributors are our key strategic partners. We don't want to alienate them by rushing into new channels." (So leave the door open to everyone who bypasses our plodding middlemen.)

"Doesn't anybody here remember what made us who we are? If it ain't broke . . . don't fix it!" (Wait for it to hit the fan to even think about what we do and why.)

It's going to take a lot to change the mind-set of those in charge. Planck's dictum says it's not likely to happen.

But by shortening the tenure of executives everywhere, speed is opening business to more fresh thinking and innovation.

Like Martha Stewart says, "It's a good thing."

#2   Equal Opportunity or Else!

The next reason we love speed: We'll finally get all the affirmative action we need . . . marketplace style.

For centuries the military promoted people because they were noble, professed a certain religion, or otherwise had the approved background.

But as British historian Brigadier Shelford Bidford has taught the American Civil War changed that:

> The best generals on both sides in the American Civil War could have probably beaten any comparable team from Europe, *for the war made the profession of generalship a career open to talent*... and freed it from the rule of authoritarians" [emphasis added].

This new faster marketplace is doing the same thing for business. Think about two of the barriers to getting ahead.

- You don't come from the right background.
- You lack sufficient experience or credentials.

Speed is demolishing those obstructions. For instance, what is the value of "experience" in today's business? Would you bet on a horse because it won the Kentucky Derby five years ago? Probably not, because in horse racing "experienced" brings to mind "old and slow."

As business moves to prizing speed over size or tenure, doesn't the same thinking apply? What makes people fast is found between their ears—not on their resume.

We tell business to ask itself some questions before evaluating any job applicant:

1. Does the job call for a great deal of problem solving?
2. Will the employee have lots of autonomy?
3. Are the things they learn *on the job* more important than the things they *bring to the job*?

4. Must they be able to learn and adapt quickly?

If they answer yes to these questions we advise them to look for attitude over experience.

In 1980, J. Walter Thompson (the ad agency) saw some attitude from a 21-year-old applicant. This kid wrote:

> I believe that technological advances in communications are on the verge of altering our way of life . . . our television becoming an information line, newspaper, school, computer, referendum machine and catalog.

But he must not have had enough experience because J. Walter passed on this young guy and his extraordinary attitude. And so Steve Case realized his dream of AOL/Time Warner without them. Bummer huh?

Case was a white guy from nowhere special (he'd sold hair care products and pizza toppings). His background was all wrong for a media mogul. And look at some of the other names in this book . . . Pujals, Bhatia, Dilsaver, etc. They are of many races, from many countries, both male and female. Central casting would never consider any of them.

But they'd be wrong. Each had all it takes for quick thinking and fast action.

So if your company restricts promotions by age, race, creed, gender, or anything else, it will certainly lose the race. And it might find itself incubating its next fierce competitor. Intel was founded by some ex–Fairchild Semiconductor guys; Charles

Schwab worked as a mutual funds manager; Def Jam Records genius Russell Simmons had a contract with CBS . . .

And those are just the names at the top. At the next level are the legions of talented coworkers who'll make their new ventures into the old company's worst nightmare.

Speed is going to do more for affirmative action than any government mandate.

#3   The Marketplace Giveth and Taketh Away . . . Now in a Hurry

The third reason we love speed: Your competitor's advantages over you will be short-lived.

Imagine we're in Washington, D.C., and it's 1940. Nationwide, Americans have been alarmed by new corporations with incredible technology and huge economies of scale. The media has forecast that these companies might stifle competition in order to preserve their position forever. So Congress has convened a "Temporary National Economic Committee" to study "the growth of monopolies and disappearance of competition due to technology and the superiority of the large over the small." But these "threats to the future of competition" have names like American Smelting, Bethlehem Steel, and Victor Talking Machine (all Dow Jones behemoths at the time). Should we tell them we've seen the future and there's nothing to worry about? (There actually was such a commission and they issued their findings in 1941. "Scant evidence size leads to monopolies," they concluded.)

Why? The marketplace giveth and taketh away . . . but now in 2002—it's faster.

Remember when Kmart was lighting up the retail world?

How about when IBM seemed immovable? Are you old enough to recall that German luxury cars were once the last word in quality and Kodak was considered an invincible monopoly. That was about the same time that the big-three TV networks (like the big-three automakers) planned on profits as far as the eye could see.

Economists since Joseph Schumpeter have taught that, as each innovation comes to market and begins to be accepted, established companies have their profits disintegrate. Capital quickly shifts to the coming thing. That shift brings more "motivation" for existing companies and entrepreneurs to up the bar again . . . and so on.

There is constant jockeying in the market as profits go to the leader, and leadership is short-lived. Today's advantage is quickly yesterday's news. Just ask Cisco, Yahoo, and Amazon . . . two years ago they looked invulnerable and now what?

And what makes it even better for those not yet at the top is that competition can come from out of nowhere. Apple, HP, and the others didn't see Dell coming. Microsoft and all the techies missed AOL. Merrill Lynch let Schwab zoom by. The big retailers must have been in meetings when both Target and H&M took a lot of the marbles.

It's always going to change and then change again. It's just that today the cycle has gone from one measured in decades to one measured in days. So if you're in the second position (or even off the radar), just you wait (and while waiting . . . get prepared)—your opportunity is coming fast.

#4 Speed Promises to Crack That Glass Ceiling Wide Open

And the fourth reason we love speed: Business will realize that women bring unique talents that are essential to quick thinking and fast action.

Business has traditionally thought and acted like a male. Corporations have been organized as a hierarchy, rewarding personalities who excel in a pecking order. And corporate decision-making has been data driven, honoring those who like to be guided by and cite "the numbers." Both are very male attitudes, derived from the way men structured their activities when they were boys.

So when women asked for equal opportunity, they got the message "become more businesslike" (in other words, think and work more like a man). Equality was confused with sameness.

Dr. Deborah Tannen teaches that a woman won't ever be more like a man. Men and women see things differently, draw different conclusions, and therefore develop different perspectives and skills. And we believe that those differences will be crucial when business decides to use speed as a competitive tool.

Hierarchies breed protocol and bureaucracies that slow everything down. People in fast organizations are decentralized and more autonomous. And autonomous people react better to influence than bossing. Women haven't traditionally been at the top of any pecking order. As youngsters they played games without losers and became skilled at using influence to get others on their side. That ability can make a big contribution to fast action.

In this book you'll read that the changes business must face have not been and will not be data driven. To have a chance of being right, fast decisions have to include understanding of the world outside our offices and an appreciation of what makes people happy. Women seek connection to everyone and everything around them. They develop feel, taste, and an intuition about what makes people happy. That gives women the skills to look beyond the numbers and empathize with people—leading them to quick thinking that is more on target.

That glass ceiling is cracked and ready to break open. Speed is going to finish the job.

THE VALIDITY OF THE LESSONS LEARNED

Twenty years ago Tom Peters and Bob Waterman, two McKinsey alumni, published *In Search of Excellence—Lessons from America's Best-Run Companies*. Their book, which detailed what they believed to be the eight basic principles of successful management, soon became the most popular business book ever published.

If you examine the fate of the companies profiled in their book, you might be tempted to question the legitimacy of their findings. IBM went into a terror-filled tailspin and would have been DOA and sold off for bits and pieces had it not been for the heroic resuscitation efforts of Lou Gerstner. HP is presently locked in a struggle for its life and at the time of this writing believes it can save itself by merging with another troubled company, Compaq. The list of companies—many of which were profiled in Peters and Waterman's book on America's best-run companies—that have fallen onto hard times or disgrace is a long one: Procter & Gamble, Levi-Strauss, Texas Instruments, McDonalds, Harris, and on and on. Others have been sopped up, merged away, disappeared, or are shadows of their former mighty selves.

Should the fate of the companies Peters and Waterman wrote about serve to discredit their findings? Absolutely not! The lessons portrayed in their book are grounded in the things the profiled companies had done to bring them to their most exalted and celebrated positions. But, as any student of business knows, most companies are like Jekyll and Hyde, capable of stunning brilliance one moment and disastrous decision making the next.

If the companies we have profiled in our book continue to do the things that got them where they wanted to be, each will survive and do well. If they don't, then all bets are off.

But one indisputable fact remains: Each of these businesses began as a small enterprise with almost no resources and proceeded to climb to a position of leadership in its respective industry. While there's no guarantee that any of the companies we have studied will continue to practice the things that got them to the top, *how* they got to the top is the real story, and the lessons we can learn from them will remain valid for many years.

In Conclusion—We Love Speed.

Speed is a force for all we believe is right about free markets and equal opportunity. And for two baby boomers (with short attention spans) it promises to keep business a lot more interesting.

Enjoy the book!

—Jason Jennings and Laurence Haughton
  Northern California, Autumn 2001
  Jason@jennings-solutions.com
  lhaughton@itsthefast.com

"We need it in the stores by tomorrow!"

Fast

"Can't you get it to us sooner?"

Faster

"Cut the damn sleeves off. We'll sell them as vests!"

Faster . . . faster

"We need your decision by this afternoon or we're taking the deal someplace else."

Faster . . . faster . . . faster . . .

"If we can't get to market faster than they do, we're dead."

Faster . . . faster . . . faster . . . faster

"Close the *effin* deal now or we're going to miss budget."

Faster . . . faster . . . whew . . . faster . . . faster

"Another $200 billion merger in our industry shocked us this morning."

Fasterfasterfasterfasterfasterfasterfasterfasterfasterfaster-fasterfasterfasterfasterfaster . . .

IT'S ALL ABOUT SPEED

Food . . . data . . . money . . . people . . . markets . . . deals . . . everything is moving at warp speed. Pick up any business magazine and you'll find a headline screaming "Speed," accompanied by the story of an executive's or company's fast climb to the top.

A single day's *Wall Street Journal* features headlines proclaiming: the need for a publishing company to act with "urgency"; Coke's promise to be more "nimble"; the U.S. Treasury secretary wagging his finger at the European Union, accusing it of growing too "slowly," and a computer maker's plans to "quickly" increase market share in office PCs. The financial and business news channels are filled with stories describing the lightning-fast ascendancy of companies, complete with graphic details of how they sopped up their slower-moving rivals.

Whatever you do, you know the new truth—It's not the big that eat the small. It's the fast that eat the slow.

EVERYTHING IS MOVING FASTER,
INCLUDING YOU—WHETHER YOU LIKE IT OR NOT—
AND IT'S ONLY GOING TO GET FASTER.

The new mantra is, "Do more with less and do it faster." Anyone unable to perform is promptly right-sized right out the door.

The bad news for some is that we're a world completely obsessed with speed. The good news for everyone ready to embrace speed is that this book will show you how to think and move faster than your competition. And, being faster doesn't mean being out of breath. It means being smarter.

We've spent the past twenty years leading our international consulting clients to their full economic potential. Along the way we've watched as companies that were able to think and move fast consistently left their competitors eating their dust. Finally, we realized, speed can be taught.

Most people, in preparation for writing a book on speed, would list those things they believe allow people and companies to move quickly and then set out on a search for confirming evidence. (Later, you'll learn about the time people spend looking for proof to defend things they already believe. It's a frightening number and it kills creativity.) We chose a different approach. We began with a blank canvas. No points to prove, no axes to grind, and no one to impress. We truly wanted to figure this "speed thing" out and boil it down into easy-to-replicate tactics.

We had to identify the fastest companies in the world, get deep inside the organizations, and find out what made them fast. Our initial list had thousands of names. Time wouldn't permit in-depth research on all of them. We had to choose. We developed the following criteria for inclusion.

Financial Metrics—The companies selected for inclusion had to "blow away" the competition when measurements of time and financial performance were compared. They had to have accomplished something big and done it faster than anyone else. We weren't interested in premature ejaculators that managed a single brief burst of speed. (Motorola designed and launched a worldwide satellite telephone network in record-setting speed . . . and then promptly plopped it into bankruptcy.) We wanted to learn from companies that had proven they could achieve speed and maintain velocity.

Relevance—The companies we selected had to have lessons to teach or business models that could be used by the readers of this book.

Access—You can't adequately research and write from the public record. If we couldn't get deep inside a company and have access to the key decision makers, we didn't include them.

Although you'll find references to companies whose inability to move fast earned them a sliding drawer in the coroner's office, we decided not to focus on them. They're yesterday's news.

Some of the companies we selected for in-depth study and from whom we gained invaluable lessons in speed are:

Charles Schwab. First, they developed criteria for making fast decisions. Second, they proved their ability to bring financial products to market faster than their competitors. Finally, they figured out the impossible—how to institutionalize innovation. The results? A company that went from four stockbrokers sitting around a single table trading stocks to the world's largest financial services firm.

Clear Channel Communications. In less than a decade, this Texas firm became the biggest out-of-home media company in the world. From 14 radio stations to almost 1,000 . . . from zero billboards to nearly 600,000. They use a unique central scoreboard to keep adding business units faster than anyone else.

AOL. In eight years, they either destroyed or devoured their much larger rivals (Prodigy and CompuServe), acquired more than eighty companies, and convinced more than 20 million Americans to send them a check every month. They began the new millennium by gobbling up Time Warner. They didn't use a vision or a mission to move fast. They launched a crusade.

H & M. Their average clothing store beats the average Gap location by more than a million dollars a year. Worldwide, they sell more than a million garments a day and have quickly grown to more than 600 locations. They defy conventional wisdom in everything they do. You'll learn how they "outgap" The Gap by staying beneath the radar and getting to market faster than anyone else.

Hotmail. A very fast rags-to-riches immigrant story. From a good idea to 20 million clients and a $400 million dollar sales price within twenty-two months. The company's founder, Sabeer Bhatia, provides lessons in seeing further and clearer and the role of innovation in speed.

Telepizza. Leo Pujals took $100,000—his entire life savings—opened a pizza restaurant, and then quickly built a $2 billion fast-food chain with 1,000 restaurants. He did in ten years what it took McDonald's seventeen to do.

Lend Lease. This Australian-based property developer and financial services firm develops and builds mammoth construction projects—including the world's most successful shopping mall and the 2000 Olympic Village—and builds them twice as fast as other companies. Their magic? A team approach and project management.

Our-in-depth study of these companies revealed twenty-five tactics that they use to think and move faster than their competitors. You can use these tactics to make your business faster, regardless of its size.

OVERVIEW

If you can't think fast, any fast action you undertake is likely to be out of haste instead of speed. In Part I, you'll learn how to anticipate the future, spot trends before others, challenge assumptions, and create an environment where the best idea wins.

In Part II, you'll discover how to blow off stifling bureaucratic structures, the value of shuffling portfolios, the need to constantly reassess everything, and how to match the decision to the consequence.

We discovered that getting to market faster than everyone else is easy. It's the "speed bumps" most companies have built that slow them down. In Part III, you'll learn the importance of abandoning traditional visions and missions and how to launch a crusade, the vital need of owning your competitive advantage, how to get vendors and suppliers operating on your timetable, the importance of staying beneath the radar, and how to build virtuous circles of speed.

In Part IV, you'll learn how to maintain velocity so that you don't end up like Toys "Я" Us. You'll learn how to use narratives and stories, how to be ruthless with resources, how to build a scoreboard that measures activity, how to stay financially flexible, the vital importance of proving the math, how to institutionalize everything, and the consequences of not staying close to the customer.

A WORD OF CAUTION: NO WHINING

During our research for this book, we discovered that being fast doesn't mean having to physically move fast (AOL's Steve Case, Lend Lease's Stuart Hornery, and Clear Channel's Lowry Mays are all pretty laid-back dudes). It has nothing to do with gender (a huge percentage of the management teams of the companies we studied are women), age, ethnicity (Sabeer Bhatia, the founder of Hotmail, was an immigrant in his mid-twenties), or educational background (many of the Telepizza millionaires never finished high school).

This book contains all the secrets and tactics used by the fastest businesspeople on the planet to achieve dizzying speed and amass huge fortunes. You can use the same tactics to become faster than you've ever hoped or dreamed of being.

BUT ... AND THERE IS A BIG BUT ...

As some people read this book, they'll find themselves muttering, "This doesn't apply to me or my business. . . . My situation is different." Unfortunately, when you scratch beneath the surface, slow people believe they breathe rarefied air, that their business or set of circumstances is unique. Hogwash! It's precisely that thinking that slows people down by stifling their sense of anticipation and their ability to innovate and improvise.

A manufacturer of printed circuit boards has as much in common with a fast-food chain as one financial services firm has with another. It's all commerce, resource deployment, and people.

So, you want to be a quicker thinker, huh? You want to move faster and reap the rewards of speed, right? Before you can begin your journey into speed, get rid of the old baggage that's slowing you down.

"It's always been done this way." Toss it. "My business is different." Stop believing that nonsense! "Our company doesn't have time to change the way we do things." If that's the case, find someplace else where your speed skills will be better utilized.

If you *truly* want to think quicker and act faster, the information is all here. You'll find real-life lessons from the fastest businesspeople and companies in the world accompanied by specific and time-proven instructions on becoming faster than anyone else. Are you *really* ready?

PART I

FAST THINKING

Speed, merely for the sake of moving fast, without a destination in mind, is haste. Eventually, out of control, speed will land you in big trouble. But imagine how many more races you'd win if you had a big head start.

Think about the advantage you'd have if you knew what the future was going to look like and were able to spot trends before the competition. Consider the power of being able to think about things quickly and accurately, tackling in minutes the same big issues and questions the competition would be processing for weeks.

Imagine for a moment the exhilaration of working in an environment where politics and palace intrigue were a thing of the past and the best idea truly wins. Such an organization would be much faster than its rivals. In this part, you'll learn how the fastest companies in the world think fast because of their ability to:

- ANTICIPATE.

- SPOT TRENDS.

- PUT EVERY IDEA THROUGH THE "GRINDER."

- LET THE BEST IDEA WIN.

ANTICIPATE

Anticipation: expecting; being aware of something in advance; to regard as possible.

*T*he ability to *anticipate* is one of the key ingredients of efficient speed. Chances are that if you just *take off* without a clear view, not knowing where you're headed, you'll end up panting, out of breath, and no better off than when you began. Maybe you'll be worse off for the exhaustion.

How can you select the right destination? How can you do a better job of anticipating what might happen, seeing the outcomes, consequences, and results in advance?

An experiment from *The Economist,* titled, "Garbage In–Garbage Out: Economic Forecasting, The Accuracy of the Dustmen's Predictions," puts the need for anticipation in perspective:

In 1984, a questionnaire was sent to four ex–Finance Ministers, four Chairmen of multinational firms, four students at Oxford and four London Dustmen (referred to in the U.S. as Garbage men).

> Ten years later the predictions were compared to the actual
> results and the British Garbage men outperformed the ex–Finance
> Ministers and the Oxford students while equaling the foresight of
> the multinational business executives on a number of key eco-
> nomic predictions. (*The Economist*, June 3, 1995)

The garbagemen did a better job of anticipating what would happen than the government officials and Oxford students. Knowing what things are going to look like in advance can help you make the right decisions. Anticipation is natural. Everyone does it every day.

We anticipate what the weather will be when we decide which clothing to wear. Moms and dads anticipate the family's transportation needs when deciding which vehicle to purchase. We even anticipate what kind of day we'll have at the office based on the gruffness or friendliness of the boss's morning greeting (or lack thereof).

Some people anticipate better than others to the extent of impacting our lifestyle. In 1953, C. A. Swanson and Sons, a poultry producer, was stuck with 260 tons of frozen turkey and insufficient storage room. They kept moving it around the country in freezer boxcars. Jerry Thomas, a salesman for the company, was on a business trip, noticed the three-compartment aluminum trays used to serve airline meals, and an idea clicked. Observing that the television was fast replacing the fireplace as the centerpiece of most American homes, he anticipated a society where the family would begin eating in the living room in front of the television. He wondered: What if you took that frozen turkey, put it into those aluminum trays alongside some stuffing and potatoes, and called them TV dinners? A half century and 6 billion dinners later, Swanson still sells more than 150 million TV dinners each year. Jerry Thomas had *anticipated* correctly.

In 1990, Leopoldo Fernando Pujals, a sales manager for Johnson & Johnson in Spain, began taking notice of the droves of women entering the Spanish workforce and reasoned they'd be too tired to cook at the end of the day. He *anticipated* the end of siestas, late-night dinners, and heavy Spanish cuisine and saw a need for home-delivered food. He founded Telepizza and ten years later was presiding over an empire with 1,000 restaurants worth $2 billion.

In 1992, Steve Case became CEO of AOL, a fledgling online service provider that counted as its customers geeks who spent their free time in the basement playing computer games. While the company's total number of customers could be counted in the thousands, Case envisioned a new world. He *anticipated* a planet where personal computers were as common as telephones and televisions, and, less than ten years later, the company he'd built from scratch gobbled up media giant Time Warner in a transaction valued at $166 billion (Dow Jones Business Wire, January 10, 2000).

Sabeer Bhatia was an Indian immigrant in the United States who spent his days watching other young computer engineers grow wealthy through their involvement in Web-based start-ups. He and his future business partner Jack Clark wanted to be rich as well. In 1996, determined to launch a company, Bhatia and Clark began spending all their free time writing the code for Java-Soft, their intended product. The duo quickly became frustrated by their inability to transfer data files between them and wondered how they could get around the fire walls designed to keep outsiders away from their respective employers' computer systems. Wouldn't it be great, they reasoned, if there were a way for everyone to have a private e-mail box? They *anticipated* a world in which everyone would have an e-mail address. Twenty-two months later, they sold their company—Hotmail—which by then had more than 20 million Microsoft clients and more than $400 million in Microsoft shares.

Unfortunately, most people limit exercising their *anticipatory* skills to daily matters such as food, clothing, and personal finances. What might happen if you could anticipate as well as Jerry Thomas, Steve Case, Leo Pujals, Sabeer Bhatia, and the other tens of thousands of businesspeople like them who have changed the world? *You can.*

NO CRYSTAL BALL REQUIRED

Who wouldn't love to be able to see the future with certainty? That would be money in the bank. We'd all know which stocks to buy, where to purchase real estate, the resources to hoard for future sale, and which businesses to bet on. Everything we anticipated would come true.

For thousand of years, scam artists ranging from the Oracle at Delphi to psychic hotlines to the Reverend Billy Bob's Divine Healing Jamboree have suckered in an unsuspecting and gullible public hoping for a glimpse of the future. The distant future cannot be seen, not even by futurists. For the last hundred years, their vision has missed a lot of what makes our world what it is. Futurists imagined electric lighting but no electric guitars, laser weapons but no laser surgery or laser disc players, giant computer databases but no Palm Pilots or video games, government surveillance cameras but no baby monitors.

We agree with Peter Drucker, who wrote, "The future cannot be known and it will be different from what exists and what we expect it to be" (*Managing for Results*). If you can't see the future, how can you anticipate?

When hockey legend Wayne Gretzky was asked what made him such a great player, he replied, "Most people skate to where the puck is. . . . I skate to where the puck is going to be." There's the difference between *anticipation* and *fortune telling*. Gretzky didn't say he skated to where the puck was going to be ten years from now or even in the next game. His greatness came from skating to where the puck was going to be a few moments from the present. That slim advantage was enough to make him the world's greatest hockey player.

Being able to anticipate that which is likely to occur in the next few months and the next few years is enough to give you an edge over 99 percent of the population who simply go along with whatever happens. Forget the far-off future. We'll get there soon enough. Leave the parlor games to the half-baked futurists, pundits, and mentalists. All you really need is a small head start—the same slim advantage Wayne Gretzky had in anticipating where the puck was going to be.

HOW TO SKATE TO WHERE THE PUCK IS GOING TO BE

As you review the following six steps, you may think they're simple. Think carefully before dismissing the simple as lacking the ability to provide a significant competitive advantage. As military historian Karl von Clausewitz observed, "Everything is very simple in war . . . but the simplest thing is very difficult."

1. ONE LOOK BACKWARDS IS WORTH TEN LOOKS FORWARD

Winston Churchill said, "The further backward you look, the further ahead you see." Don't misunderstand what he was saying. He wasn't promoting the typical organizational look backward—the one where business takes account of the past five years and plans for more of the same in the future. That kind of forecasting has been completely discredited.

Churchill was urging that those who want to know the future first assemble a thorough recognition of the past. Looking back at the epoch trends and great themes of humanity, he was saying, improves your ability to imagine what will be.

While in Madrid, Spain, doing research for this book, we asked the hotel concierge for directions to the head office of Telepizza. Inquiring as to the nature of our business with Telepizza, we told him we were going to interview the company's founder, Leopoldo Pujals. In hushed, almost reverential tones, the concierge explained in great detail what a great man Pujals was, adding, "How lucky Pujals was to have seen the future."

What the hotel concierge didn't know was that Leo Pujals wasn't a native Spaniard but had been born in Cuba, fled with his family to Florida, spent his teenage and college years in the United States, and had witnessed firsthand the explosion of fast, take-out, and home-delivered food in the 1960s and 1970s. Pujals wasn't lucky. He hadn't seen the future. He had a good memory.

Become a history buff. Make some time for serious reading of what has gone before. Chances are good it'll happen again. For example, history shows that during the early years of the twentieth century department stores killed the local general merchants. Then, in the 1970s, department stores had to fight for their lives against malls and discounters. In the 1980s, shopping malls and the 1970s-style discounters were threatened by the category killers and the big-box stores. Now, all business categories are threatened by the dot coms.

All of these changes have been propelled by the same dynamic: the costs of connecting communities and commerce. First, department stores were made possible by the revolutionary impact of the railways. (Transporting a ton of goods could once quadruple the selling price of an item, but with rail the costs dropped instantly to one-twentieth of their former level.) Lowered costs led to lowered prices, larger scale led to economies, faster distribution led to increased inventory turn, and it all led to success for national and regional department stores.

Then malls and big-box stores were fueled by another economy in connecting customers with products: the advent of highways, cars, and the move to the suburbs. Consumers could drive to an outskirt location and get even more choices and better prices. Focus and lower prices led to even greater inventory turn.

Now the Internet shows another connection between communities (buyers) and commercial offers (sellers) that allows for inventory turns of as much as 25 times yearly. This means gross profit margins as low as 5 percent could net returns on investment similar to a 40-percent margin in a department store that turns its goods four times annually.

Through this bit of history you discover that the biggest disruption of existing retail models comes about as new connections between community and commerce reduce the costs of inventory and increase turn (something the folks at H&M are currently using to be the fastest in their category with an eight-time inventory turn).

2. WHAT'S THE NEXT LIFE CYCLE?

In 1996, Raymond Smith, the chairman of Bell Atlantic, said in a speech that the process of absorbing a revolutionary technology takes about thirty years and comes in four phases:

1. The invention itself.

2. Key-enabling technologies converge to spread the invention.

3. The key insight that turns a technological possibility into a new way of communicating.

4. Business models emerge that direct investments and channel creative talent to the service of an unmet market need.

To Smith's list we add a fifth phase:

5. Consolidation prevails. This occurs when the product or service becomes so commonplace and is offered by so many companies that price wars erupt, the product or service becomes a commodity, and consolidation becomes inevitable, with no more than three suppliers remaining.

We agreed with Smith in 1996, and still do, but now we doubt that the cycle will take thirty years—it may become lightning fast.

If you want to know where the big innovations and successes will be in your business, figure out where the business is right now and anticipate the changes that will occur when the business moves to its next phase. Chances are the same things will happen and the same opportunities will be present that faced every other business that moved from one life cycle to the next. History is on your side.

3. QUESTION EVERYTHING . . . ALL THE TIME

Sabeer Bhatia, Hotmail's founder, credits his ruthless questioning of everything as the source of his creativity and ability to anticipate. Shortly after his arrival in the United States, Bhatia received a very low grade on a university paper he submitted. He was crushed. The experience turned out to be life-changing. Bhatia tells a story with which almost every former student can identify:

> My entire education had been gained in a knowledge-based system. You are taught things, you learn everything from a book, and then at exam time you repeat it. When I was asked to write my first paper, I read all the books on the subject and basically rewrote the whole thing. When I received the low grade, the teacher explained that the purpose of writing a paper was to add to a body of knowledge, not to regurgitate it.

That experience caused Bhatia to resolve to accept nothing as presented and to question everything. In doing so, he even became a fan of Big Macs:

> In Hinduism, the cow is considered sacred and beef is never eaten. I wanted to know why. Nobody seemed to know. I kept questioning until I found the answer. I discovered that in the early days the cow was more valuable for its dairy products than its meat. As centuries went by, people started singing songs of praise to the

rivers, the sun, nature, and ... the cow. It just became accepted that Hindus don't eat beef. Because I dared to question, I can eat lots of Big Macs without guilt.

Bhatia adds, "If you want to hone your anticipatory skills, accept nothing. Question everything. Ask how and why of everything that's presented to you."

4. STOP WORKING FOR YOUR BUSINESS—
WORK ON YOUR BUSINESS

Most businesspeople are so busy working for their business or in their business that they never find time to work *on* their business. Thus, they fail to anticipate what might happen or what they might be able to make happen.

For the past several years, we've served as the keynote speakers for a series of Asian conferences attended by business owners, CEOs, and managing directors worldwide. For four days, with all mobile telephones and pagers turned off, they learn from some of the best business practitioners and teachers in the world and have an opportunity to engage in private meetings with members of the faculty. During these sessions, participants are encouraged to talk about why they went into business, how they view their business, and where they'd like to take their business.

For a few days, instead of dealing with tardy employees, bad information, unhelpful vendors and suppliers, and accounts receivable and payable, they're encouraged to be aspirational and anticipate what customers really want. One man—not from the United States—who we met at one of the conferences in Indonesia, owned a company whose business was installing television antennas. Over the years he'd made a fortune, but he knew that cable and satellite television would soon render his business obsolete. All his frantic attempts to win contracts for installation of satellite dishes had failed. Unable to find another use for the vast infrastructure he'd built, he was on the verge of closing the business.

He was so busy working in, and worrying about, the fate of his business that he hadn't asked himself what other businesses he could be in. When we began prodding him about what else was happening in the cities he served, he became uncomfortable, at one point exclaiming, "I'm here to find out how to stay in business, not talk about urban culture." We kept pestering him with questions until he finally exploded, "The cities I serve are hell holes, like all other cities, filled with rising crime rates and unhappy people."

QUESTION: What historically follows a rise in crime rates?
ANSWER: An increase in the installation of burglar alarms.

QUESTION: What do you need to install burglar alarms?
ANSWER: A fleet of vehicles and technicians.

QUESTION: What did this man's company already possess?

Today, he's out of the antenna business and into the burglar alarm business in a big and profitable way. The real question is: How could a smart person who many would describe as street savvy not have seen the potential earlier? He'd been so busy working in his business and for his business that he'd stopped observing the world. When you stop looking, you lose the ability to *anticipate* what might be.

Observing daily life and wondering what might be and how you and your company might play an integral role is far too important to be viewed as an extracurricular activity. Time constraints and the demands of day-to-day business make it almost impossible to hang a CLOSED sign on your door for any substantial length of time, and, to further complicate matters, the need for downtime, recreation, and family time means most weekends are already spoken for. Our advice flies in the face of conventional work ethic wisdom. Based on personal experience and observation, we recommend spending at least one full day each month out of the office doing nothing but working on your business. (One day a week would be even better.)

Here's a list of questions you need to ask yourself each time you spend a day working *on* your business. By the time you answer our questions, dozens more will have occurred to you:

- What is the real potential for the business unit?
- Do you need to be offering other products/services to achieve your full potential?
- Would offering other products/services take your eye off the ball?
- What is your *real* BIG objective?
- How quickly can this objective be achieved?
- Is there anything that should be destroyed or abandoned?
- What additional human and financial resources would be required to achieve your big objective?
- Do you have access to those resources?
- What would you do with the wealth created?

- How badly do you want to achieve the big objective?

- What are you willing to invest (time, money, other resources) to achieve it?

- How quickly could the big objective be realized?

- Do you have the right people in the right positions to achieve the big objective?

- How many more customers do you need to achieve the big objective?

- What does each customer need to spend in order to achieve the big objective?

- Is the world changing faster on the outside than you're changing on the inside?

- Are there divisions/department/product or service lines that should be dumped?

- Are you strong enough to make those decisions and implement them?

Unless you regularly schedule time away from your business to consider your responses to the previous questions, you'll never achieve your big objective and it will remain an elusive dream.

5. BECOME A SCENARIO PLANNER

Intel's Andy Grove has a rule: "Only the paranoid survive." Paranoid people believe someone or some force is out to get them. In business they'd be right. There are a lot of things to worry about. Everyone and everything is indeed out to get you.

The "what ifs" are endless. What if your current product line doesn't sell? What if your top performer is recruited by the competition? What if traffic in the stores stalls? What if the sales leads dry up? What if the bank doesn't extend the credit line? All effective leaders or managers constantly ask the "what if" questions. To not ask them assumes a continuation of the present and reveals the leader or manager is extremely naive.

Scenario planning is an institutionalized exercise in forward thinking. A small group of people from a company get together and ask the "what if" questions and create a series of possible strategic and tactical responses. It calls on other talent within the organization to start doing some of the big thinking.

A few years ago, the managing director of one of England's largest banks gathered his top people for a scenario planning session and asked: "What would our response be if one of the other large British banks opened a branch tomorrow in each of our markets?" The assembled executives came up with a lengthy list of initiatives that could be undertaken including widespread cost reductions. It was, after all, only an exercise, and some of their suggestions were extraordinarily bold and included changes in their own compensation programs.

As the day wrapped up and everyone was engaged in back-slapping and self-congratulations for an exercise well done, the managing director took the microphone and announced that one of their large competitors wasn't about to open a branch in each of the cities they served, at least not soon, but nonetheless, in order to be prepared, all of the sweeping initiatives the executives had put forth would be implemented the following day. Within the next twelve months, the bank became Britain's most profitable.

Gary Hamel, management guru and author of *Competing for*

the Future, points out that most corporate executives spend less than 2.4 percent of their time actively thinking about the future. Based on a fifty-hour workweek, that's less than fifteen minutes a day. In fact, many corporate bigwigs boastfully point out that they *never* hold formal meetings to discuss the future but do it on the fly whenever they can spare a few moments. We can only guess that these same people have their secretaries print out their e-mail and then they handwrite or dictate a response so that the secretary can e-mail a reply. Guidelines for scenario planning include:

- Schedule sessions as regular meetings. Don't do it on the fly.

- Schedule sessions at least once monthly.

- Allow several hours for discussion.

- The head of the operating unit—you—should always be present.

- Sessions should be inclusive and diverse. Someone from the assembly line will often have more to contribute than one of the suits.

- No more than twelve people should attend each session.

- A specific project should be assigned a small group with a deadline for submission of recommendations.

- Members should change frequently.

- The leader should begin by painting a vivid picture of a possible event or series of events.

- A history of recommendations and actions should be kept.

6. HAVE EMPATHY

Read the next paragraph closely. Read it over and over again until you fully understand the meaning of the word *empathy*. If you aren't able to understand empathy, you won't be able to use one of the most powerful anticipatory weapons in your arsenal.

Empathy is the ability to be aware, sensitive, and vicariously subjected to the feelings, thoughts, and experiences of another without having the feelings, thoughts, or experiences fully communicated in an explicit manner. In short, empathy lets you know what it feels like to be in someone else's shoes. Consider the following:

There is a new book-selling competition and everyone is alarmed. "Our sales will plummet! We can't compete. Everybody is using them. Every customer is talking about it."

Who is this new competitor? Amazon.com? Nope. The year was 1854 and the competitor was . . . Free Libraries. The booksellers had every right to panic. Consider the advantages of Free Libraries:

- They were publicly funded and cost-free for the user.

- They were open to everyone.

- They had every book and periodical.

- They stored the books and loaned them to you when you wanted them.

Now, consider the bookselling business at the time:

- Books were expensive.

- If you owned books, you had to store them.

- There was nothing to do with the books once you read them.

Why didn't Free Libraries destroy the bookselling business? People prefer things for free, don't they? You only spend a limited amount of hours reading a book. Why are people so irrational as to prefer buying a book to borrowing it?

Now, put your empathy in overdrive. Consider book buyers empathetically. Reach deep inside yourself for an understanding of why people buy books. People want to own knowledge and it's worth a lot to them to do it on their own terms. Plus, those bookshelves at home announce to the world that you're a person of knowledge. That's why people buy books: to own knowledge and have others see them as people of knowledge.

How can you become more empathetic? By being truly interested in others and encouraging them to tell their story and share their view of the world. As they do, listen and observe carefully. You can consciously reach deep inside yourself and work to experience the emotions of the other person.

During a training session we were conducting for a group of new advertising sales executives, we were relating the story of a man we'd spent time with the previous day. He owned a large electronics store. In the middle of the discussion about advertising, he appeared to become distracted. Sensing something was wrong, we asked, "Are you okay? You seem to have left the conversation." He sighed deeply and said, "Damn! Here we are talking about advertising and I don't have enough money in the bank for next week's payroll and loan payment. I'm so preoccupied I can't think about anything else."

We asked the group if they could understand what he was feeling. A brave, young, recent university graduate raised her hand and said, "No! How can I know what he was feeling? I've never owned a business. I've never worried about meeting a payroll. How could you expect me to know?" We asked her if she had ever worried about money. She said of course she had: money for tuition, books, and car payments.

Empathy is the ability to reach deep inside, find a similar experience or set of emotions, and allow yourself to feel like the other person. We've found that when you're able to successfully communicate that you do understand what the other person is feeling, she'll open up, tell you everything, and once she has told you the answer, she'll swear you're a mind reader for knowing it.

[A SIXTY-SECOND HEADS-UP]

Become more skilled at anticipating by:

- Looking backward to see forward
- Figuring out the next life cycle for the business
- Questioning everything
- Starting to work on the business, not in the business
- Regularly conducting scenario planning workshops
- Developing your sense of empathy

SPOT TRENDS

Most people use research the same way a drunk uses a lamppost—for support rather than illumination.

David Ogilvy, Confessions of an Ad Man

*B*esides being able to anticipate, the ability to spot trends before others is an important weapon to keep in your arsenal if you want to think faster than your competition. Historically, business, with a chronic addiction to research and focus groups, has a lousy batting average when it comes to spotting trends and making decisions about what will work, what won't, and the creation and introduction of new products and services. By an alarming margin, they get it wrong.

Only 1 out of 671 new products ever hits its sales or profit forecast (Robert Macmath, *What Were They Thinking*). You'd be fired with that kind of record. Remember the predictable result when Gerber, the baby food people, introduced adult-sized portions called "Singles for Adults" in clear glass bottles with names like creamed beef, chicken madeira, and turkey mornay? (Yuck!)

What about Iridium, the ill-fated worldwide satellite telephone service? What trends were the folks at Motorola spotting when they decided people would be willing to lug a three-pound telephone around the world, be forced to go outside to use it (the phone wouldn't work inside buildings), point the phone's antenna at the azimuth as if they were baying at the moon, and then, on top of everything else, pay $10 per minute for a crackly connection?

Businesses' track record in *not* recognizing trends that have real potential is abysmal too. In the early 1980s, McKinsey Consulting forecast that the worldwide market for mobile telephones would top out at 900,000 by the year 2000 (*The Economist* August 9, 1999). As a result, AT&T pulled the plug on their involvement. Yet, by this time, 900,000 people around the world were signing up for mobile telephones every three days! (AT&T eventually and expensively made a belated return to the fray.)

The steps we recommend for becoming a master trend-spotter include:

- UNDERSTAND THE DRIVERS OF CHANGE.

- GET A CLUE.

- LOOK FOR NEW COMBINATIONS.

- DEVELOP A SENSE OF TASTE.

I. UNDERSTAND THE DRIVERS OF CHANGE

Trends in business are almost always led by one of five broad categories called drivers of change.

CUSTOMER-LED DRIVERS include the changes in market make-up such as demographic shifts, income alterations, and attitudinal moves in demand, for example, changing definitions of value and convenience.

TECHNOLOGY-LED DRIVERS are the advances, due to engineering innovation or breakthroughs, that occur in either the primary or enabler industries. One of the examples that made Wal-Mart so dominant was the leap forward in information storage and networking. Without these advances, their real-time data use (second only to the U.S. government) would be impossible.

CAPITAL-LED DRIVERS include the change brought on by the institutional investor and the resultant alterations in standards of performance. EBITDA (Earnings before interest, taxes, depreciation, and amortization) wasn't on the lips of most of us a decade ago and the idea of paying $12,000 per customer for an acquisition (Vodafone in a recent deal) was unheard of.

Consider the 500 new publicly traded Internet competitors with overflowing war chests and no demand for current quarter (or year) profitability and you can see how capital-led drivers dramatically affect the playing field.

GOVERNMENT-LED DRIVERS include all the legislative mischief and policy initiatives that can impact business. From employment issues, tax policy, liability, and loophole incentives, the invisible hand of politicians makes a dramatic impact.

COMPETITOR-LED DRIVERS are the easiest to imagine as business executives spend almost all their forecasting energy asking "what if" about their challengers. Still, they make an impact, especially the new entrant, who often is not saddled with the same constraints as the incumbent.

As you're reading and researching news on the Internet, newspapers, and magazines, consciously remember to ask yourself: Will what I'm reading eventually constitute a driver of change?

2. GET A CLUE

In 1999—the year is an important part of the story—we were asked to consider taking on a large electronics retailer as a client. The task would be to help them figure out what to do regarding the Internet. A first meeting was scheduled.

It began with the CEO admitting that he knew his stores needed to be on the "Internationlnet" (his word, not ours) and he was prepared to spend $500,000 doing it, but he demanded a return on investment before he'd go further. As he continued with his pontificating opening comments, we got that all-too-familiar sinking feeling in our gut. He was, as our friend Guy Kawasaki would say, a Bozo.

Looking around the room filled with twelve company executives, we were struck by another awful truth. They were all white males in their fifties. What the hell had we gotten ourselves into? Unless we could find a way to bail fast, it promised to be a long day.

We started with a few questions. We asked how many had e-mail addresses. Only the CEO had one and he admitted he didn't know how to access his mail—his personal assistant did it each day. Next, we asked how many of them had ever "surfed" the Net. None had, but a few boastfully proclaimed their kids knew how. Then, wondering where the $500,000 figure had come from, we asked the group how much it cost them to open a brick and mortar store. With the help of vendors and suppliers, they agreed, it was between $5 million and $7 million.

Finally, what kind of store, we wondered, could they hope to open for $500,000? Their reaction was unanimous. "You can't open a store for $500,000. You can hardly fixture a store for that." Kerplunk!

It's alarming how many business decisions, collectively involving hundreds of millions of dollars, are made each day by business executives who are clueless. After twenty years of being in, studying, and consulting businesses around the world, it's our observation that there are three types of businesspeople: those who make things happen, those who watch things happen, and those who wonder, "What in the hell just happened?" If you want to be among the small group who make things happen, you'll have to learn to recognize trends.

HOW TO SPOT TRENDS FIRST

Use the Internet. For years, we've argued that society is quickly evolving into a new set of "haves" and "have-nots." The "haves" possess the ability to manage, store, manipulate, and move data. The "have-nots" are the computer illiterate.

The Internet is the best tool that's ever been available for observing life and identifying new communities. Spend at least an hour daily on the Internet and you'll quickly be discovering new communities and trends. Consider it vital work, not an indulgence.

Read. The average American subscribes to 1.6 magazines. Unfortunately, most often their selections mirror their interests. Engineers subscribe to engineering publications, sports addicts to sports magazines, and so on.

Unless you subscribe to a large and diverse group of publications, you're missing the opportunity to identify new opportunities and trends. Given the cheap price of magazine subscriptions, it's inconceivable that anyone wanting to be a trend-spotter wouldn't subscribe to twenty or thirty magazines. At an average annual subscription rate of $20, subscribing to thirty diverse magazines would set you back $50 a month. You don't need to read everything—simply leafing through and ripping out the items that catch your eye is sufficient.

Study the gay community. Buffed bodies, cargo pants, thick black shoes, body piercing, dance clubs, hot travel destinations, and the gentrification of urban neighborhoods are just a few of the recent trends that began in the gay community. If you don't have gay friends, make a few. If you don't have gay employees and advisors, hire some. If the mere idea bothers you, see a shrink and find out why.

Seek other communities. For as long as civilization has existed, community has preceded commerce. What are the new and emerging communities you could be serving or selling to? Are there lots of people who are techno literate but without sufficient financial resources to acquire their own computer?

The entrepreneurs who quickly opened the thousands of storefronts across Australia, Asia, and Europe, housing row upon row of computers available for rental by the hour, spotted a new community and are making fortunes.

Was there a huge community of people who believed that grandma's old junk in the attic and garage was worth lots of money? E-bay seems to have proven the point.

Listen to music. For one week in the autumn of 1999, the word *sex* was replaced by another term as the most searched item on the

Internet. During the next few months we addressed hundreds of CEOs and managing directors and always asked how many knew the term. A hand never went up. "C'mon," we'd constantly implore. "Somebody here has to know . . . what is it?" Not a single hand was raised. None of these business chieftains knew the term *MP3*—the new format of downloaded music from the Internet.

Get yourself an MP3 player or just download music right to your computer. Listen to radio stations that play new music. Ask your kids about the singers and groups they're listening to. Ask people what they want. Dave Pottruck, co-CEO of Charles Schwab, says that most of Schwab's huge innovations have come from asking customers questions. "What can we do better?" "How can we make your life easier?" "What new service or product would you like to see us offering?"

When you find common themes in response to your questioning, it's a certainty someone will be addressing those concerns in the form of a new product or service. The asking of questions should be done by all levels of the organization but *especially* by those at the top.

In most companies, customer contact is, unfortunately, either outsourced or left to those low on the food chain. When these folks come up with great ideas and initiatives—and they do—by the time the idea reaches the executive suite, all the idea's sharp edges have generally been whittled away by the old guard (if not stolen entirely by some dufus). Because only the people at the top have the ability to significantly change an organization or quickly deploy the resources required for big bold initiatives, it's imperative that people at the top be in regular and direct contact with customers.

Travel. The stupendous potential for wireless telephony and Internet access was obvious to anyone who took the time to visit

Europe, Scandinavia, and Asia during the mid- to late 1990s. Upon the realization that nations without huge copper wire infra-structures would never build them, it became easy to connect the dots and see the wireless future.

With the exception of fast-food hamburgers and juice bars, vir-tually every other trend in dining originated in countries other than the United States. Those who traveled and experienced local cul-tures were the fortunate individuals who scored big. Even the inspi-ration for Starbucks came from its founder's love of European coffeehouses. Anytime you're fortunate enough to score an inter-national air ticket, take it and spend a few extra days walking the streets and watching what's happening, particularly with the young.

Watch the box. Not long ago we were dining at the home of a CEO of a large HMO. Conversation turned to the television pro-gram that had for months taken America by storm: "Who Wants to Be a Millionaire." The faces of both the CEO and his wife went blank. They didn't have a clue as to what everyone else was talking about. The best they could muster up is that they didn't watch tele-vision, preferring to listen to classical music. It was like announcing to the rest of the dinner table that they had their heads stuck up a certain part of their anatomy.

You can't know what's happening in the real world unless you're watching MTV, VH1, the Star music channel, and the hun-dreds of commercial networks. You can't predict what consumers are thinking and what they want if you aren't watching the same television commercials as them. And it's impossible to have any idea of fashion if you aren't studying what clothing people are wearing. Television, streamed video, and video games should function not as much as entertainment but as your window on the world.

Study how people live. In most nations, Saturday or Sunday is when real estate agents hold open houses for prospective home purchasers. If you're organized, you can visit ten to fifteen homes in a day. What an incredible opportunity.

Unless you're in the market for a new home, forget the house and study what's inside. How have the homeowners used the space? Which areas of the house are the most lived in? What kind of furnishings do they have? What kind of floor coverings? What packaged foods are in the pantry and cupboards? What kind of recreational gear is hanging in the garage? How many video monitors are there? How many computers are there? What colors have they used in decorating? It won't take long before you're able to make a few connections and land on trends such as hot tubs and media rooms.

Tom Freston, CEO of MTV Networks (responsible for Nickelodeon, VH1, TV Land, and tons of MTV programming) has said, "I think if we can be totally connected with our viewers . . . get inside their heads and get inside their closets, their CD collection, and translate that, along with a lot of internal intuition, into a product, everything else in our business will fall into place."

Read the streets. With a shaved head and goatee, thirty-four-year-old Fabian Mansson is the former CEO who spent several years guiding H&M, the hottest and fastest-growing chain of fashion retailers in the world. Opening an average of 3 stores each week, the firm's 600 stores sell more than a million garments a day, and, in every measure of financial performance, H&M "outgaps" The Gap.

The H&M design staff never attend fashion shows. Instead, they hang out in the pubs, bars, and clubs, attend sporting contests, watch parents with their children, go to rock concerts, eat in restaurants, and study the streets for their next season's line of merchandise.

3. LOOK FOR NEW COMBINATIONS

It's what you learn after you know it all that makes you smart. There was a martial arts studio in Chicago that opened to sell tae kwon do lessons to the neighborhood. The owner/instructor was a lifelong adherent to the philosophy of martial arts. He was tough, exacting, and demanding. Mothers in the neighborhood loved the service he provided. What do you think the mothers were buying?

- Was it self-defense training for their children who had to survive on some very mean streets?

- Was it an after-school babysitting service?

- Was it to build the self-esteem and self-confidence of their children?

- Was it none of the above?

According to the mothers, it wasn't about martial arts training, babysitting, or self-esteem. They all noticed that, after just a few sessions, their children were crisply answering "Yes Sir" and "Yes Ma'am" when asked a question. The kids came home and more diligently addressed their homework. They took out the trash with just one request. They were more *disciplined*.

The mothers weren't buying tae kwon do lessons. They were

buying discipline. Imagine how pricing and additional services could have been affected had the owner made the connection between what he was selling and what the mothers were *really* buying.

As most managers progress in their careers, they become focused in their specialty. Unfortunately, most veteran executives, even those who have crossed several internal departments, tend to see the world only through the lens of their area of expertise.

> Chuang-tse, a sage of ancient China wrote about the downside of being a specialist: "A well-frog cannot imagine the ocean, nor can a summer insect conceive of ice . . . (each) is restricted by its own learning."
>
> —B. Hoff, "The Tao of Pooh"

When you gather these experts to consider the future, you get a room full of croaking about what each of them knows. IBM passed on the chance to invest in Xerox Corporation because they saw the market for dry copiers as replacements for the photocopying machine. Restricted by their own learning, they couldn't imagine the hundreds of new applications that users would find as the cost and availability of Xeroxes came into line.

We tend to associate creativity with the arts and to think of it as the expression of highly original ideas. In business, though, originality isn't the objective. To be creative in business, an idea must be useful and actionable. Often the most creative things in business put existing ideas together in new combinations. Business creativity and the ability to see new combinations depends on discovering answers outside an individual discipline.

As Charles F. Kettering, who invented the first ignition system and went on to head GM's research laboratories for more than thirty years, commented, "An inventor is an engineer who doesn't take his education too seriously."

One exercise we've found to be effective is answering the question: What are customers buying from you? in terms that don't include the name of the service or product or any insider jargon but in words that anyone, in any field, could understand.

Mary Parker Follett initiated our thinking with her "Law of the Situation." In the early part of the twentieth century, Ms. Follett wanted to open the minds at a window shade maker to new possibilities. So she proposed that the company wasn't in the business of manufacturing blinds and shutters but rather was in the *lighting-control* business. By categorizing business using the customer's point of view, she created a new perspective for the decision makers. (One that might encourage them to listen to a salesman offering electrical lights and rheostats instead of telling him "that newfangled technology will never replace good old blinds.")

Ted Taylor decided lettuce buyers weren't really buying lettuce. They wanted salad and he figured out how to get it to them. Leaving the families' traditional lettuce-growing and distribution business, he founded Fresh Express. He washed and chopped the lettuce, tossed in a packet of dressing, and sealed it all in a bag that kept the salad fresh for weeks.

To spot trends and take advantage of them before your competition:

- Define your business in simple, generic, and relevant terms.

- See your product or service from the eyes of the consumer.

- Connect products and services with the function they serve in the customers' current pursuit of self-interest.

4. DEVELOP A SENSE OF TASTE

Research didn't predict the success of the telephone, radio, television, cable, personal computer, fax machine, or mobile telephone. In fact, research "proved" that none of them—along with theme parks, hotels on Interstate highways, and fast-food restaurants— would ever have financial success.

In the case of each venture, someone had sufficient *taste* to recognize its potential value and either anticipated the possibilities or spotted a trend on which to capitalize.

> **taste:** *critical judgment, discernment, or appreciation; to grasp the nature, worth, quality, or significance of; to judge with heightened perception or reality.*

Fundamentally, taste is sensitivity about what pleases and helps make people happy. How does one develop taste? Watching what makes others happy. Learning what makes others unhappy. Observing what pleases people. Understanding what displeases people. Knowing what gives people joy. Understanding what makes you happy. Being in sync with the customer. Or as the CEO of MTV Networks concluded about his success: MTV has "a dedicated staff of young employees who genuinely like their customers' taste."

To quote a famous chef on what it takes to become a great cook, "Let yourself be led by your palate, your tongue, your eyes, and your heart."

You'll find yourself thinking faster than the next person when you understand the primary drivers of change, work at staying plugged in, constantly search for new combinations, and work on developing a sense of heightened perception.

[**A SIXTY-SECOND HEADS-UP**] ➡

In order to become a better trend-spotter, make certain you:

- Understand the drivers of change
- Get a clue
- Look for new combinations
- Develop your taste

PUT EVERY IDEA THROUGH
THE "GRINDER"

*T*he ability to anticipate and spot trends won't help you move faster or ensure your success unless you develop the skills required to quickly assess an idea's potential for success. In our study of the world's fastest companies, we noticed many things that most had in common. But, without exception, one trait that was always present was the ability to ruthlessly, quickly, and accurately assess the potential for success for new products/services, prospective acquisitions, and new business opportunities.

In stark contrast to the prevailing belief that speed is about tossing the dice and the consequences be damned, we found the fastest companies on the planet use another approach.

MINIMIZE THE RISK OF FAILURE. ONLY THEN,
CONSIDER MAXIMIZING SUCCESS.

*START BY PUTTING EVERYTHING
THROUGH THE "GRINDER."*

In a column for *Forbes* magazine on the subject of business plans, Guy Kawasaki, co-founder of Garage.com and the author of *Rules for Revolutionaries*, wrote that entrepreneurs should never use Chinese math in their plans. "Chinese math," Kawasaki explained, "is when you invoke China's 1.4 billion citizens in your plan by forecasting: If we succeed in getting just 1 percent of the population to buy our widget, we'll have a huge success."

Most businesspeople are consistently guilty of overestimating the ease with which a huge objective can be achieved and underestimating the resources (the time, people, and money) required to achieve it. If you want to think faster than everyone, put every idea that comes your way through the "grinder"— the twelve questions distilled from studying the world's fastest companies. The answers you end up with will determine if you have a winner or a dud.

I. DOES SUCCESS RELY ON THE GREATER FOOL THEORY?

The greater fool theory presumes there's always someone else dumber than you who will bail or buy you out. For example, when you buy the hot shares of an Internet company, ignorant of the risks associated with speculative investing, believing there will always be someone willing to pay more than the amount you paid, you've bought into the greater fool theory.

Perhaps there was a time when P. T. Barnum's dictum, "There's another fool born every minute," was true. Today, information is in the process of becoming completely democratized by the Internet. Whether it's the actual price an automobile dealer paid the manufacturer for a car or the academic credentials being claimed by a dermatologist pretending to be a plastic surgeon, everything's there for anyone to learn. The number of dumb people is quickly diminishing. If the idea being considered is predicated on a marketplace filled with fools, the fastest and smartest companies will take a pass on the deal.

2. WILL YOU BE SWIMMING UPSTREAM?

Sometimes an idea or a deal comes along that has potential, but . . . *it's just too hard.* Fifteen years ago, we met a veterinary researcher who thought he'd landed on what he considered to be a novel and inexpensive device for inoculating cows against a rare bovine disease. Using Chinese math he was convinced he was about to make a fortune. (After all, if there are 1.4 billion people in China, how many cows must there be in the world?)

Not long ago, we bumped into him again. He was still working on his invention, claiming he'd make millions someday. When we inquired as to how things were going, he delivered a scathing attack on the drug manufacturers that, he claimed, had locked him out, the bureaucrats who wouldn't approve his device for use, and the banks that refused to fund him. By this time, he'd lost his house, wife, and kids, his clothes were frayed, and he'd given up employment for occasional part-time work in veterinary clinics.

Although the ability to hang in there can be an admirable one, at some point you've got to know when to pull the pin. How hard is it going to be? Who will be your allies and who won't? Who will be working against you? Are there self-interests and resources greater than yours? Many people fizzle away precious time and resources trying to push uphill. The fastest people don't waste their time swimming upstream.

3. ARE YOU BETTING THE RANCH?

In less than a decade, CEO Mark Mays and his brother, CFO (chief financial officer) Randall Mays, transformed Clear Channel Communication, a small radio group of 14 stations, into the world's largest out-of-home media company with nearly 1,000 radio stations and more than 600,000 billboards. They maintain their ability to be opportunistic is one of the primary reasons for their success and cite a clean balance sheet as the reason they've always been able to fund their growth. Similarly, when you examine other companies that have demonstrated the ability to move fast and maintain velocity, you'll find clean balance sheets. Clear Channel steadfastly refuses to imperil the company by biting off more than they can chew.

When AOL went public in 1992 at $13 a share, they raised $20 million—hardly enough cash to fund the billions of dollars in acquisitions they would make during the next eight years gobbling up scores of companies. CEO Steve Case's secret was never using his cash hoard to acquire other companies. Instead, he convinced the owners of businesses he wanted to buy to give him their firms—and their technology—in return for AOL shares. If one of Steve Case's acquisitions didn't work out, AOL would have survived.

If a single deal or decision could place the business in jeopardy, it isn't smart to do the deal—it's stupid. The fastest and smartest businesspeople will leave that deal for someone else who is trying to work out a testosterone problem and will pick it up later at a bargain-basement price.

4. HAS SOMEONE PROVEN THE MATH?

Due diligence is the process that a company undertakes between the time it enters into an agreement to purchase another firm and the date the deal closes. This is the company's opportunity to make certain it's getting exactly what it agreed to buy.

With much gusto and vast expense, the due diligence team (generally a combination of company executives assisted by high-priced talent from a big 5 accounting firm) is dispatched to count inventories, audit books, check cash balances and accounts receivable, and make certain the deal is okay. Although the importance of having the bean-counters shouldn't be discounted, we're not aware of a single due diligence team that's bothered to do the most important math:

- What does it cost the company to acquire a customer (counted in time, people, and money)?

- How much will that customer spend?

- How much will be left over after costs and debt service?

When Leo Pujals took his life savings and opened up the first Telepizza restaurant in Madrid, Spain, his first order of business— after creating a great product—was proving the math. Within a few months, he'd figured out exactly how many advertising fliers had to be distributed each day to sell the number of pizzas he wanted to sell.

By experimenting and fine-tuning the questions that callers were asked—"Would you like extra cheese with that?" "Would you like garlic bread with your pizza?"—he was able to determine precisely the revenues he'd achieve each day.

As Pujals says, "The first restaurant was hard. We had to prove the math would work. After that, it was easy. How many restaurants do you want to have? 100? 500? 1,000? 5,000? Once you know the math, it's just a matter of plugging it in."

Because Pujals took the time to prove the math, he was able to grow from 1 restaurant to 1,000 within ten years . . . besting the seventeen years it took McDonald's to do the same. The smartest and fastest companies in the world realize that if you can't prove the math, you're taking a shot in the dark.

5. WHAT'S THE BACKUP PLAN?

Not every idea, deal, or initiative works out. In all the fast companies we studied, there's always a backup plan. On January 1, 2000, the market capitalization of Charles Schwab surpassed that of Merrill Lynch, and Schwab became the world's largest financial services company. Not bad, considering that only a few years earlier Merrill Lynch had dwarfed Schwab by a margin of 100 to 1.

Dave Pottruck, co-CEO of Schwab, knows that every idea and decision won't be the right one when he says:

> The idea that failure is okay is ridiculous. I'm not going to go around the company and reward somebody for failing. Here at Schwab we deal with the concept of *noble* failure versus *stupid* fail-

ure. Noble failures are when you have a good plan, you've thought everything through carefully, have a contingency plan to deal with any initial failure, implement with discipline, and implement the contingency plan if required.

The fastest thinkers always have a contingency plan. Trying to come up with one later, when something isn't working as planned (and few things go as planned), slows you down.

6. WILL IT BE A GOOD THING EVEN IF . . .

Unless someone's just fallen off the back of a turnip truck, he knows it's almost impossible to predict the exact results of a business decision. You would need a crystal ball for that.

Sometimes we're pleasantly surprised. Perhaps demand for a new product or service so exceeds our forecasts that everyone on the team looks like a hero. But more often than not it's the other way around.

Demand isn't what we thought it would be . . . there were cost overruns and it appears the fat margins promised the suits aren't going to happen . . . the conversion rate of inquiries to closed sales is out of whack, and everything that could go wrong did.

The backup plan was implemented and it still failed to achieve the desired results. It may be time to bail, cut your losses, shut it down, move on, start over, or employ your capital (time, money, and resources) in another way. But something else we discovered in our study of the fastest companies in the world was that even if they failed to achieve their ultimate objective, something beneficial was achieved.

Liddell Hart wrote "take a line of operation which offers alternate objectives" as one of his eight guiding principles for military success. As the generals consider the likelihood of the mission's success, they do sufficient scenario planning to make certain that even if they fail in their stated objective, they'll be in a better place (with their troops safe and their resources where they want them) than they were before and better positioned for the fight to follow.

When a quick thinker is considering an idea, he or she always asks the question: Even if this fails to achieve what I think is possible, are we better off than before?

7. WILL IT SIDETRACK YOU?

Sabeer Bhatia was only able to raise $300,000 to take Hotmail from conception to launch. Initially, Hotmail was going to be a consumer product. As the firm quickly grew from Bhatia and his partner to twelve engineers, most of whom were working for nothing more than company shares, the plan expanded to target three markets: consumer, business, and a proprietary business e-mail product.

Bhatia believes that many businesses fail by trying to do too much too soon with too few resources. Early in Hotmail's existence, a potential customer—instant cash—appeared. It was seductive, but as Bhatia explains, "When you have twelve engineers and you're trying to go after three different markets, and one of those markets has a potential deal on the table, but in order to get it done you'd have to pull two people off your core product, you take your focus away and end up with no leverage."

Most start-ups with no income would have leapt for the chance at a quick cash transfusion, even if it meant taking their eye off their core product. If Bhatia had taken the deal waiting on the table, Hotmail, as the world knows it, might not have come into being.

Bhatia offers a metaphor to explain how he thinks fast: "It's like driving down the freeway and finding the path of least resistance and deciding which lane will give you the maximum leverage. You have to be constantly asking yourself: Which of these three lanes will get me the farthest ahead without getting caught in traffic?"

From the day he took over the helm of AOL, Steve Case made it clear that his company wasn't going to get sidetracked by becoming involved in businesses they knew nothing about. They were a content provider, not a technology company. AOL's unprecedented (at the time) acquisition of Netscape wouldn't have taken place unless Case had been unable to unload the technology parts of the company on Sun Microsystems.

Imagine the problems Hotmail might have faced had they continued to chase three markets with less than $300,000 in capital. Consider how screwed-up and out of hand things might have become if Case had had to deal with running a technology company as well as a content provider.

Fast thinkers always ask: Will what I'm deciding cause me to lose focus on the big objective? If there's a possibility that it might, the idea is deep-sixed.

8. CAN IT BE DONE FOR LESS?

Assume that when someone is pitching you a proposal or an idea, it's likely she's presenting a budget filled with fat, her pet idea, or both. Fast thinkers don't waste their time on a first-draft proposal that includes spending precious capital or operating money. A terse "Go and rework the numbers and come back to me with something other than a fairytale" is generally enough to let the other party know she'd better sharpen her pencil.

Our study of the fastest thinkers and movers in business led us to a new guiding principle:

RADICAL COST CUTTING OFTEN LEADS TO SURPRISE IN INNOVATION.

When Lou Gerstner was hired to revive the fortunes of IBM in 1993, he promptly slashed the R&D budget by $1 billion. There was the predictable wailing and gnashing of teeth. Hundreds of scientists left and one physicist lamented, "All the infrastructure I built up over fifteen years was destroyed."

Those who stayed focused less on blue-sky projects and honed in on product matters. Scientists began spending more time with product developers and customers through First of a Kind, a research project that pairs existing research projects with a prospective IBM customer and tries to solve a real-world problem. Gerstner's program of doing it for less set off a surge in breakthroughs including speedier chip technology, voice recognition systems, and radical improvements in hard disk storage.

Each time an idea/project comes across their desk that requires money, fast thinkers first ask: Can it be done for less?

9. IS IT DÉJÀ VU ALL OVER AGAIN?

WHAT WERE THE UNEXPECTED FAILURES THE LAST TIME?

The fast thinker has a good memory, learns from previous experiences, and always learns from failure including the unexpected failures that occasionally take place. Clear Channel Communication notes every operational decision they make and then keeps assiduous track of the outcomes. Not only is the same mistake never repeated a second time, but the company is also able to raise the issue of the unexpected failures experienced the last time around.

Every time a company decision backfires or one of its initiatives fails, the following questions should be asked and the answers recorded for future reference:

- What were the unexpected failures the last time we did something like this?

- Did we learn something we can capitalize on this time?

- What's changed this time around?

- Why won't the same failures happen again?

- Did our failures keep us from achieving what we set out to achieve?

- How much effort might I/we waste dealing with failures?

WERE THERE SURPRISE SUCCESSES THE LAST TIME?

Sometimes nice surprises happen. When American Express introduced their new blue card featuring a hologram, smart technology, and a personal card reader, they were buried with requests for the card, and within the first year had signed on more than one million users—double the number they'd anticipated. It was a nice surprise.

Fast thinkers learn from their past successes as well as their failures, and ask:

- What were our unexpected successes the last time we did something similar?

- Did we learn something we can capitalize on this time?

- Did we leverage what we learned the last time around?

- Was it just the nice surprises that got us where we wanted to be?

- Will success this time require nice surprises?

Even the success American Express enjoyed with the blue card causes fast thinkers concern in the form of three questions:

- Who in the hell was in charge of the research that showed they'd only issue 500,000 cards?

- Was somebody sandbagging to make himself look like a hero?

- What other numbers have been missed by 100 percent?

Most companies make each decision independent of one another, basking in the glory of the decisions that work out and conve-

IT'S THE FAST THAT EAT THE SLOW

niently forgetting those that don't. When a business fails to record and learn from its unexpected failures and successes, it is doomed to making the same or similar decisions over and over again—like a gerbil on a toy wheel—without having learned anything. This slows down the decision-making process.

10. OOPS...IS IT A SNAPPLE DECISION?

Quaker Oats bought Snapple for billions. They spent hundreds of millions trying to make it work. In the end, they lost more than a billion dollars that rightfully belonged to the shareholders.

Why did they buy Snapple? It was a pure case of outlandish corporate ego. The Quaker Oats folks thought they could sell anything, especially a trendy (at the time) drink product.

Quaker Oats proceeded to make every mistake that could be made, and a few years later, with their collective tails tucked firmly between their suits, they quietly disposed of the company at a huge loss. Their egos bit them in the backside.

Ego is a luxury that business can ill afford. When putting potential projects through the "grinder," you must ask: Is this proposition purely a business play or have egos gone awry? Resources (time, knowledge, and money) are precious and must be reserved for the deal(s) with the biggest potential economic payoff.

11. ARE THERE BARRIERS TO ENTRY FOR OTHERS?

Is there any way to keep out the competition? That's one of the first questions that smart, fast people ask of any business idea.

When you study how Clear Channel quickly assembled their media empire, you can't help but notice they've only selected businesses with high barriers of entry to others: radio, billboards, and concert and performance venues. There aren't any more commercial radio licenses being issued in the United States and any competitor would find it nearly impossible to duplicate Clear Channel's lineup of 1,000 stations. Similarly, almost every nation has passed legislation prohibiting new billboards but "grandfathering" in existing locations. When you quickly purchase companies and consolidate more than 600,000 faces, it's unlikely you'll face significant competition.

Can you own most or all of the current capacity providing you a head start?

- Is there a patent prohibiting others from manufacturing or selling?

- Can it be copyrighted and belong exclusively to you?

- Is it the last piece of buildable land?

- Is there legislation dictating there won't be any more of a certain practice?

- Is regulatory approval so difficult to receive that few would consider the time and expense involved?

- Is the capital required so large that no one would be likely to put that much at risk?

Fast thinkers are always asking if the idea or plan being considered allows for the existence/creation of barriers that make it hard for others to enter the business.

[A SIXTY-SECOND HEADS-UP] ➡

If you want to be a fast thinker with a winning track record, follow these steps when considering a decision:

• First, figure out how to minimize failure.

• Then, put every idea through the "grinder" and ask the following questions:

  • Does success rely on the great fool theory?

  • Will you be swimming upstream?

  • Are you betting the ranch?

  • Has the math been proven?

  • Is there a backup plan?

  • Will it be a good thing even if...?

  • Will it sidetrack you?

  • Can it be done for less?

  • What were the unexpected failures and successes the last time?

  • Is it an ego play or a business play?

  • Are there barriers to entry for others?

THE BEST IDEA WINS

*I*t only makes sense . . . Of course, the *best idea* should win. It shouldn't matter whether it comes from someone on the assembly line, the sales department, a temporary worker in the mailroom, or one of the suits in the executive suite. But creating an environment where the best idea—*regardless of origin*—wins is an art not yet mastered by most companies and it prevents them from thinking fast.

Evelyn Dilsaver, a senior vice president and the driving force behind innovation at Charles Schwab, reminds us of a basic business truth when she says, "Big ideas and innovation come from the top because that's where the resources are and that's where the power to say *yes* exists. Most often it's only the chair or the CEO who can push an idea with sharp edges through the company."

Unfortunately, in most companies, on the journey from the starting place to the executive suite, a lot of potentially great ideas suffer one of the following fates:

It's hijacked. Often, in businesses with multilayered management structures, by the time a potentially great idea makes it up the ladder, it's been stolen by some jerk who has never had an original idea in his life and relies on stealing other people's ideas to ensure his tenure. When that happens, workers and associates retaliate by keeping good ideas to themselves. When ideas get hijacked, an organization's thinking begins to slow down.

The magic vanishes. Schwab's Dilsaver adds that, "When you're forced to pass your idea up through a hierarchical structure, everyone negotiates away the sharp edges and it gets honed down to something that doesn't mean anything." When all of the sharp edges of an idea or suggestion are constantly taken away, people become discouraged and state they either don't have the time or the interest in putting forth their ideas. The business's thinking becomes even slower.

It's deep-sixed. Someone decides the idea has no merit—in actuality the idea threatens him or her—and the idea is conveniently forgotten. The seeds for destruction of the organization have been sown.

When workers witness ideas being hijacked, changed so that they don't resemble the original idea, or deep-sixed, they quickly conclude it isn't worth the time or energy to contribute their ideas. The quickest companies employ six tactics to ensure they keep thinking faster than their rivals.

CREATE AN ENVIRONMENT
WHERE THE BEST IDEA WINS!

I. CHECK YOUR EGO AT THE DOOR

As we traveled the world studying fast companies, the difference between *ego* and *ego trip* became increasingly obvious. If ego is about individuality and self-esteem, then the leaders of every fast-thinking company we uncovered had more than a healthy dose. But if ego is defined as being devoted entirely to one's own feeling and being, we found none.

Dr. Norman Dixon, author of *On the Psychology of Military Incompetence*, studied centuries of failed leadership in the face of fast change and big consequence. He concluded that the common link among incompetent decision makers was in their "authoritarian patterns of behavior." These patterns were demonstrated by anti-intellectualism (an inclination to pontificate, an aversion to feedback that threatens self-esteem, and a compulsive attraction to rank and deference), anti-effeminacy, shows of macho bravado, unwillingness to compromise, prizing brute strength over cognitive skills, and displays of infantilism (throwing tantrums, exploding irrationally, and a disregard for the difficulty their decisions forced on those around them).

The reason many business managers and executives are unable to create and nurture a collaborative environment—one where the best idea wins—is because they suffer from these same "authoritarian patterns." There are clichés in the hundreds giving testament to the fact that a company is only as good as its human capital, and one business leader after another is quoted as saying the sole reason for their success is the more talented people around them. In reality, such proclamations have more to do with spin than practice and belief.

Until managers get over the misguided belief that only they or their cronies can have a truly inspired idea or that *their* idea must be the best one, there's no way an organization can think . . . and subsequently move fast.

2. GIVE EVERYONE A VOICE, THEN LISTEN

Most executives say they listen to employees, but this isn't the case at slow companies. More typical is the conduct exhibited by the former CEO of a troubled Internet B2C organization.

The company was once a high-flying dot com. In January 1999, their share price was kissing the $40 mark. Twelve months later, it had fallen 90 percent and the CEO called the troops together for a breakfast meeting to ask: What's not working? Presumably he was interested in collecting the thoughts of the employees. As the employees put forth a list of stinging answers and gripes, he lashed back with: "Eliminate the whiners. I'm serious . . . maybe it's better if they looked for another job" (*Wall Street Journal*, December 10, 1999). That CEO really didn't want to listen to the ideas people had to offer.

Managers who are serious about thinking fast must establish and maintain a dialogue with every level of the organization. Every manager should have a special e-mail address, widely publicized to associates, workers, and customers, for the express purpose of receiving suggestions and ideas. The leader should personally review and acknowledge every message received, with no well-intended and protective assistant acting as a middle person and doing the filtering.

In response to those who think they wouldn't have time to

review and respond to all the messages they'd receive (ugh . . . talk about ego and inflated self-importance), we'd offer up Andy Grove, chair of Intel, and Dave Pottruck, co-CEO of Charles Schwab, both of whom respond to *every* e-mail every day.

3. MAKE LOTS OF SALES CALLS

There's no more effective way of becoming a quick thinker and creating an environment where the best idea wins than by regularly spending time in the field with salespeople and customers. Not long ago, the general manager of a large group of radio stations we were consulting agreed to make five sales calls weekly with his sales staff. Two months later, citing a busy schedule, he still hadn't made one. We asked him what he would do if he were ordered by the CEO to make the calls. He responded, only half jokingly, "I'd have to kill myself."

Most businesspeople think that by the time the lofty title of manager is bestowed on them, they've been emancipated from the hard work and fear associated with making sales calls. Their contact with sales is generally limited to the occasional celebratory lunch (when the real work has already been done) or the annual golf day.

Evelyn Dilsaver of Schwab explains what happens when you don't have intimate knowledge of the front lines:

> Look, at most companies, half the time the stuff that people in the field and branches do the executives never find out about. Imagine what can happen when you latch on to it and legitimize it. It's potentially awesome.

One of the old rules at Schwab was that our front-line personnel were prohibited from recommending a financial advisor even if the customer needed one. Our reasoning was that we hadn't done the due diligence and hadn't sorted out the legal structures of such recommendations. So, we actually fired people if they recommended an advisor. They did it anyway.

Finally, when the executives realized it was happening and wasn't going to stop, we did the necessary work and created Advisor Source™, which now refers more than $1.2 billion quarterly in assets to advisors. The problem is that it took us two years to get it done. What might the financial impact have been had we thought and moved even faster?

If Lou Gerstner, the quick-thinking CEO who turned around IBM, is able to spend half his time making sales calls, observing, and discovering big ideas, so can you.

4. REWARD BIG IDEAS

During the record-setting building of Hotmail, Sabeer Bhatia tossed around options like confetti and allowed everyone the chance to become rich. He says that the real issue behind people not improvising and offering up their big ideas is one of insufficient incentives.

"I'm aware of many large companies," Bhatia says, "where they give you a check for $500 or $1,000 and a plaque to hang on the wall saying COOL IDEA. That kind of money doesn't cut it for people anymore. If you want a constant flow of big ideas from your people, then you must reward them in a bigger way, give them stock in the company, a vested interest in achieving the vision of the company."

Practicing what he preaches, when Bhatia sold Hotmail, half the people working for the company became millionaires—not bad for less than two years' work.

5. CREATE PROJECT TEAMS

American business has long embraced and glorified the Horatio Alger rags-to-riches mentality. The good news is that when you have a nation of 270 million educated people working independently with access to cheap capital, their sheer numbers ensure huge amounts of innovation. The bad news is that when people spend most of their time working alone in an environment where individual victory is seen as superior to group achievement, people run the risk of becoming self-centered and possessive about "their" ideas.

Lend Lease is an Australian engineering, construction, and financial services company that routinely builds huge challenging projects on budget and in half the time of their rivals. To ensure that the best idea wins, the company uses a team approach to every project. According to company chair, Stuart Hornery, "When you bring all the interested parties together, provide them a set of specific objectives, and monitor and support their progress, you leave little room for ego and lots of space for the best ideas to be put forth."

Another very fast company, whose guiding principle is: "Act fast," is TII Industries, a manufacturer of surge-protection equipment for the telecom industry. Each morning COO (chief operating officer) George Katsarakes conducts a twenty-one-minute teleconference with the company's seventy key leaders and managers around the world. The purpose of the meeting is twofold: Make certain nothing slips through the cracks and foster a sense of urgency.

Functioning like a large project team, the group is asked the same three questions each day. Did anyone get hurt anywhere yesterday? Are all of our customers happy? Are there any hot issues—whether good or bad—at any of the plants? The handling of a hot issue is assigned to someone with the expectation that it will be resolved by the next day's meeting.

6. ACKNOWLEDGE PEOPLE'S CONTRIBUTIONS EVERY DAY

Numerous studies have demonstrated that when people love their jobs, the amount of money they earn is fourth, fifth, or sixth on the list of what's important to them. Alternatively, when people hate their jobs money is predictably number one.

People seek acknowledgment and validation. Nothing feels better than a public pat on the back and a handshake. If you want to create a fast-thinking environment where people eagerly share their suggestions and ideas, make it a daily ritual to publicly commend workers for their thinking.

It's tough being in charge. There are always lots of daily crises and it's generally the problems—not the wins and the victories—that come to the manager's attention. If a manager wants to make the transition from manager to leader, he or she must actively seek out the good news and then publicly acknowledge those responsible.

If you dig deep enough, there is good news every day at every company. The late author James Kirkwood offers some delightful advice for finding something good to talk about. Kirkwood tells the story of two identical twin boys. One is always happy and the other is always depressed. Finally, frustrated and at the end of their ropes, the parents take the boys to a psychiatrist who assures them he can "even out" the boys' dispositions.

He places the sad little boy in a room filled with toys and the happy little boy in a room filled with manure. Giving the parents a knowing wink, he assures them that all will be well. An hour later, the shrink and the parents go to the first door and open it. There atop a rocking horse sits the sad little boy, still unhappy and crying great big tears. Next, they march down the hall to the room where the happy little boy has been locked up with a pile of manure. As they open the door, they hear exuberant shouts. They look into the room with amazement and see the child on top of the manure pile throwing handfuls into the air, shouting. "Whoopee! With all this horse poop, there has to be a pony in here someplace!"

A daily responsibility of leaders who wish to create and foster an environment where the best idea wins is to find the pony buried in the manure and publicly acknowledge and thank the pony.

[A SIXTY-SECOND HEADS-UP]

- Every day, consciously remind yourself to set your ego aside. Acknowledge that good ideas exist at every level of the company.

- Give everyone within the organization a voice and direct access to you.

- Get off your butt, hang out with the salespeople a minimum of two days weekly, and make real sales calls. (This will be the single most monumental achievement you'll ever accomplish. Despite their bravado to the contrary, most managers are afraid of customers and are frightened to make salescalls.)

• Loosen the purse strings and generously reward people for big ideas.

• Create project teams to come up with new ways to achieve each corporate objective.

• Find a pony every day and proudly parade it around the company.

PART II

FAST DECISIONS

*F*ast thinking won't get you very far unless you're able to quickly process your thoughts and make a decision. Nothing slows down an organization more than paralysis by analysis—the inability to make even the smallest decisions quickly.

If you follow the tactics explained in this section, you'll be speedily making scores of correct decisions while your slower-moving rivals are still convening meeting with human resources to "process" their thinking. Imagine how much easier life would be if you had a simple set of guidelines—*shared by everyone in the organization*—for making decisions. The fastest-thinking businesses have such a list.

Think about how much faster decisions would be made if you didn't have endless layers of bureaucratic nonsense to wade through daily. The fastest-thinking firms don't have bureaucratic structures.

Consider the ease of decision making if the company was filled with capable and experienced multiskilled individuals. That's why the fastest-thinking companies shuffle portfolios.

Finally, ponder how personally freeing it would be to realize that every decision doesn't have to be the right one. Sometimes it's okay to make the wrong decision.

In this part, you'll learn how the fastest-thinking companies in the world make fast decisions:

- RULES FOR FAST DECISIONS.

- BLOW OUT THE BUREAUCRACY.

- UNBUNDLE EVERYTHING.

- SHUFFLE PORTFOLIOS.

- CONSTANTLY REASSESS EVERYTHING.

RULES FOR FAST DECISIONS

*R*emember your last business decision? Maybe it was adding a new menu item or product line. Perhaps it was about pressing the *go* button on a new technology project or accepting a piece of business for fewer dollars than you'd hoped.

In the process of wrestling with your need to make a *fast* decision, did you reach for a list of guiding principles? Is that a smirk? The fastest decision makers in the world use a formal set of guiding principles to make *all* their decisions.

The reason slow thinkers are unable to make quick decisions is that each represents a move into uncharted waters . . . without benefit of a tide map. In order to understand the role that guiding principles play for the fastest decision makers, a history lesson is required.

A QUICK HISTORY LESSON

Remember mission statements? A single-page document filled with more platitudes than you'd find in a prayer book spelling out the business's mission. No one remembered the darn things, it was business as usual, and the document didn't have the profound impact on the fortunes of the business its creators had hoped for. The mission statement exercise was quickly forgotten.

Then came the 1990s and . . . every company needed a vision. A new name. . . . the same old silly exercise.

All the worker bees exchanged winks and knowing glances. The suits would have to be indulged one more time. In 99 percent of all cases, the same result—having a vision—changed nothing.

HISTORY REPEATS ITSELF . . . AGAIN.

Today, the new fad is the rush to craft sets of corporate values or guiding principles. And again the exercise will be a complete waste of time for most businesses.

The guiding principles of most companies are created in the same way that missions and visions were crafted. Months are spent . . . executives are nominated, countless meetings are held, reams of recommendations are reviewed, everything is processed and then processed some more.

Finally, an exclusive team of executives led by the head of HR go into retreat to accomplish the serious work awaiting them— the creation of a list of principles that will guide the company. Upon completion, the guiding principles are unfurled for the troops, published in the annual report, and framed for viewing in the reception area. Then . . . nothing happens.

For the vast majority of companies, nothing will be different. The exercise will have wasted time and talent.

DO AS I SAY . . . NOT AS I DO.

Several years ago, the general manager of a business unit of one of our clients proclaimed a new guiding principle: the *democratization* of the workplace. "No more private offices," he announced. "Our new facility," he proudly bellowed, "will nurture innovation and improvisation by breaking down walls and barriers."

Of course, the jerk neglected to mention that plans for the new building had everyone *hot-desking* it . . . except himself. His private office came complete with private bath, separate sitting and meeting areas, and a minibar.

There was a revolt of the troops and eventually he left (his arrogance had manifested itself in other ways) with his tail tucked between his legs, still insisting he'd been misunderstood. Unless *everyone* in the organization knows the guiding principles, practices them, and is *seen* practicing them, they are an utter waste of time and ultimately a demoralizer. They will slow you down . . . not speed you up.

Tactically, a set of guiding principles has value and makes you faster only if they do the things their title implies.

> **Guide**—*to lead, show the way, direct the movements of . . .*

> **Principles**—*a law that serves as the basis of reasoning and action, a personal code of conduct . . .*

Most companies spend needless hours, days, weeks, even months anguishing over whether a tactic should be deployed, a product or service should be introduced, and which course of action to take. Then, after they've made the wrong decision, countless time is spent recycling decisions and doing it all over again.

Fast—as opposed to hasty—companies that have demonstrated the ability to sustain surge and velocity all have sets of guiding principles to help them make quick decisions. When a company is prepared to abandon their lofty, theoretical, and politically correct "values" in favor of a practical, down-to-earth list of guiding principles, the decision-making process becomes lightning fast. Only one question need be asked of any proposed course of action: Does it fit our guiding principles?

In quickly building the world's largest financial services company, Charles Schwab was guided by a simple set of principles, and every company initiative, new product, or new direction is forced to pass the test.

SCHWAB'S GUIDING PRINCIPLES

- Is it fair and responsive to our customers?

- Does it respect our fellow employees and the spirit of teamwork?

- Are we striving relentlessly to improve what we do and how we do it?

- Will it earn, and will we be worthy of, our customers' trust?

- Will it reinvent the business?

- We are willing to risk short-term revenue to do the right thing for the customer and ensure long-term success.

- Will we own the technology?

- Does it leverage the brand to build trust?

- Will it create and nurture a spirit of innovation?

At Schwab, by the time a question has been framed and asked, the answer becomes evident simply by asking one question: Does what we're proposing to do fit the firm's guiding principles?

By late 1994, Dave Pottruck, president and co-CEO of Charles Schwab, and Chuck Schwab, the firm's founder and chairperson, believed that online trading was going to become huge and a project code named Project Hawk was created. Because the firm owned the technology (remember: one of their guiding principles is to always own the technology), within months the technology group was ready to present a product to the brass.

Schwab says that when he saw the demonstration of someone entering an order on a PC, having it move through all of Schwab's sophisticated mainframes, executing a trade, and e-mailing back a confirmation, he fell off his chair. Schwab and Pottruck didn't require lengthy discussion and hand-wringing about when to introduce their new product. Two of their guiding principles—reinventing the business and constantly improving what they do—answered for them.

Acting with lightning speed, the firm debuted e.schwab in May 1996 and all hell broke loose. The company signed up 25,000 customers within two weeks—their target for the full year.

For a while, Schwab had their cake and ate it too, as they offered two separate products: the new e.schwab online product where customers paid a flat $29.95 per trade and regular online accounts where customers were charged 20 percent less than if a Schwab rep did the deal.

By 1997, there was discontent underfoot. Schwab's front-line personnel weren't fans of e.schwab, believing it took business from the branches, customers were confused about the dual pricing structure, and they wanted both full service and $29.95 trades. In the autumn of 1997, Pottruck sat down with Schwab and they decided to end the dual pricing structure and merge e.schwab into the organization. There would be one company and anyone could make a trade for $29.95, online or off, and take advantage of the company's full array of services.

Most executives wouldn't have made the same tough call as quickly as Pottruck and Schwab. All the other brokerage companies could have done the same thing, but instead, as late as 1998, Merrill Lynch derided the Web as a passing fad and didn't think or decide fast enough.

When Pottruck and Schwab made their decision, the firm's average commission was $65 and internal documents showed that by moving to flat-rate pricing the company could take a first-year financial hit of $125 million. Ultimately, the decision wasn't a tough one for Pottruck or Schwab. They had their list of guiding principles and one of them stated that *they would be willing to risk short-term revenue growth if it was right for the customer and ensured long-term success.*

Quick decision making paid off for Schwab. By the start of

2000, Schwab had an average 25 percent market share, was handling one of four stock trades in the United States, was receiving nearly 80 million hits on peak days, had opened up more than 3 million online accounts, and was doing more than $10 billion weekly in e-commerce.

Lend Lease, another one of the fastest companies in the world, has no problem making big decisions quickly. The company builds some of the most spectacular structures in the world, is a leader in the insurance and mutual fund businesses, and is involved big time in the computer business.

In 1996, Stuart Hornery, Lend Lease's chairperson, and Malcom Latham, tribal elder, visited London, stood on a patch of land, and stared at a huge industrial wasteland that had stood vacant for years. Without much discussion they made a fast decision. They would do what no other company had been able to do: transform a former chalk pit into the most stunning and successful shopping mall in the world.

Their fast decision was fed by one of their guiding principles—*to do what no one else has done.* In only 1,618 days, Lead Lease bought the property, totally abandoned the approved design and crafted an entirely new one, won government approval, signed leases with more than 320 of the world's leading retailers, and built Bluewater, a 1.6-million-square-foot treasure boasting 50 acres of parks, seven lakes, more than 1 million trees, and more than 80,000 shoppers a day.

They did the Bluewater project like they do all their projects— ahead of schedule, under budget, and fully leased. For more than forty years, the company has maintained a 24 percent annual increase in their share price—*it's another guiding principle*—a track record accomplished by no other company.

Hornery, who has led the company for twenty years, sums up the role of his company's guiding principles when he says:

> If our guiding principles are genuinely held and practiced throughout the company, we will attract the best people to work for us, the quality of our work will attract the attention of customers, demand for our services will grow, and our global family will prosper—all of which contributes to delivering superior value for shareholders.

THE LEND LEASE GUIDING PRINCIPLES

- Dare to be different in everything we do—the enemy of mediocrity.

- Never do anything that would diminish the pride our parents have in us.

- No nasty surprises—grow earnings every year.

- Be a leading employer.

- Enhance the environment.

- We need special relationships to enhance our capabilities.

- No individual has a monopoly on good ideas.

- We will only prosper with the support of the communities with which we interact.

- We wish all employees to be shareholders.

- We believe there is a strong link between good governance and performance.

At Lend Lease not a single decision is made without the decision maker consulting the firm's guiding principles.

WHAT IF THERE AREN'T ANY GUIDING PRINCIPLES WHERE YOU WORK?

If leaders and managers within an organization don't have a set of guiding principles to help them make *fast* decisions, they'll make them in one of three ways:

By the seat of the pants. If the organization is fortunate enough to have a highly intuitive leader capable of making quick decisions without benefit of a set of guiding principles, the organization may be lucky as long as that person remains in her position and her streak of luck continues. History demonstrates that organizations headed by such charismatic/lucky seat-of-the-pants operators are generally thrown into upheaval with the demise or departure of that person.

Pick a tactic—any tactic. When a business doesn't have a set of guiding principles, it's presumed that anything goes . . . that any tactic can be employed to achieve a stated objective. The problem with this scenario is that there are simply so many tactics to consider that valuable time is wasted thinking, considering, studying, questioning, debating, and pondering a course of action. The reason most organizations are slow is because they spend too much time sprinkling water on fires that were started by having recklessly chosen the wrong course of action in the first place.

What's in it for me. Unless a company has a set of guiding principles for fast decision making, the tendency of the decision maker will be to ask: What's in it for me? rather than: What's in it for the company? When a company makes a decision this way, there's big trouble looming.

WHERE DO GUIDING PRINCIPLES COME FROM?

Ideally, guiding principles come from enlightened CEOs, managing directors, department heads, or business owners who understand the need for a tool to be used in making fast, consistent decisions in concert with his or her ethics and beliefs. Guiding principles are a statement of the leader's view of the world—how he see things, what he believes is right and wrong, moral and immoral, the role of the company in the community, the importance of customers, employees, vendors, and suppliers.

In the interest of fostering inclusiveness and gaining the "buy-in" of those around them, skillful leaders involve others in the creation of the guiding principles as long as none of the principles adopted violate their beliefs. If a leader enlists the talents of others to create the guiding principles he or she should reach beyond the executive team and involve people from every level of the organization.

HOW ARE GUIDING PRINCIPLES ENFORCED?

Guiding principles are *lived* first and then enforced. Charles Handy, in *The Age of Unreason*, says, "It tempts credulity to proclaim a campaign for the homeless from a penthouse apartment." We agree.

First, the leader must be seen as making fast decisions in accordance with the principles that have been proclaimed. Only then has he or she earned the right to expect others to use the same set of principles in making speedy decisions. Eventually, making any decision not in keeping with the firm's stated principles becomes a firing offense, with violators quickly removed from the business unit.

IF YOU DISAGREE WITH YOUR FIRM'S GUIDING PRINCIPLES...

If you strongly disagree with your company's guiding principles, you have three options:

Fight to change them. If your worth to the firm, in dollar terms, is of sufficient importance, you'll have a good chance of changing the principle(s) with which you disagree. If you're low on the totem pole and your contribution can't be measured in dollar terms, you'll probably be seen as a whiner and you'd probably be better off leaving.

Sell out and suck up. One of Bizarro's great cartoons shows the big boss at the head of a conference table babbling and surrounded by a half-dozen underlings. The boss's dialogue balloon shows a picture of a fierce lion—the way the boss views himself. All the other dialogue balloons have the rear view of a horse—the way everyone else views him. If you're able to exchange your guiding principles for a paycheck, you'll have joined millions of unhappy and cynical people who have done the same.

Leave. Charles Schwab founded his company because he was offended by the way the company where he worked treated their customers. Leopoldo Pujals founded Telepizza because Johnson & Johnson denied him a promotion he believed was promised to him.

Steve Case's soul wasn't fed working for Pizza Hut and trying to figure out the best pizza toppings. People whose previous employers didn't share their view of the world start most entrepreneurial ventures. Maybe it's your turn.

For most companies, the creation of a set of guiding principles will have as little impact as did their mission or vision. They'll be placed in a frame, plastered on the wall, and occasionally and vaguely referred to until they're replaced by the next management fad. Accomplished leaders, managers, and executives who need to think and move fast recognize the need to embrace and use guiding principles as a vital decision-making tool.

THE RESPONSIBILITY OF THE LEADER/MANAGER

It's incumbent of any leader or manager who wishes to create an environment filled with people who are fast thinkers and operate in the best interests of the company to:

- Create and publish a set of guiding principles

- Be seen as making all decisions consistent with the stated guiding principles

- Make certain everyone reporting to you knows the guiding principles and is empowered to make decisions compatible with them

- Discuss the guiding principles frequently

- Not publicly acknowledge or reward people who make decisions that violate the stated guiding principles even if one occasionally achieves short-term revenue

- Terminate those people who consistently violate the guiding principles in making decisions

WHAT ARE YOUR GUIDING PRINCIPLES?

1. _____

2. _____

3. _____

4. _____

5. _____

6. _____

7. _____

8. _____

[**A SIXTY-SECOND HEADS-UP**] ➡

- Most companies use guiding principles the same way they used missions and visions—as silly time-wasting exercises.

- The fastest decision makers use a set of guiding principles to assist them in making every decision.

- Guiding principles have no value unless everyone knows them and uses them in making fast decisions.

- What are your company's guiding principles?

BLOW OUT THE BUREAUCRACY

Bureaucracy: government by central administration, a nation or organization so governed; the officials of such an organization, regarded as oppressive and inflexible.

*B*lowing out the bureaucracy shouldn't be a chapter in a book. It should be a law! Anyone found guilty of building or perpetuating bureaucracies should be tried on charges of *management malpractice*, found guilty, and spend serious time in the slammer.

We've never found an organization with a large bureaucracy that was able to make fast decisions. The more dead weight at the top of the organization involved in the decision-making process, the slower the decisions will be made.

DON'T B.S. YOURSELF

One of our mentors was Bill Pfifely, a former accomplished CEO of the Bank of California, who took us under his wing and guided us during our early years in business. Once we asked him for the single most important piece of business advice he could offer. Without pondering for a moment, he responded, "Sometimes in life you'll have to bullshit your customers and let them think everything is okay even if it isn't. It's not right, but it happens. Sometimes you'll have to bullshit the people who work with you and let them believe everything is okay even if it's not. It isn't right, but it happens." Then came the zinger:

"But show me someone who bullshits themselves and I'll show you someone who will be a complete failure."

Most company executives and managers B.S. themselves when it comes to knowing whether they've created or are nurturing a bureaucratic mess incapable of fast decisions.

We agree with Clear Channel Communications CFO Randall Mays when he says, "Everyone says they're decentralized and don't have bureaucracies. Bullshit! Most companies—*including our competitors*—who call themselves decentralized are actually top-down autocratic companies. Our secret is that our people run their own businesses and make all their own decisions."

TAKE A POP QUIZ: DO YOU HAVE A BUREAUCRACY?

What about your company? Answer the following questions:

- Are decisions made at one central location?

- Is the answer "I have to check with 'so and so' " frequently used as the response to a request for a decision?

- Is the phrase "I'll need to see what the higher-ups think about it" used often?

- Are there special executive committees for making even easy decisions?

- Must human resources approve every decision?

- Do they think they should?

- Do you hear the word *process* tossed around a lot?

- Is the word *empower* talked about more than it is practiced?

- Are there enough executives to have office politics and palace intrigue?

- Does it require more than one conversation to get a decision or an explanation of how the decision will be made?

If you're able to answer yes to any of the questions, chances are you've created, manage, or work in a bureaucratic organization.

WHERE SHOULD FAST DECISIONS BE MADE?

In order for decisions to be fast and correct, they should be made as close to the *real* action as possible. If it's a sales issue, the decision should either be made by the salesperson or sales manager. If it's a production problem, the production manager should make the call. If it's a potential acquisition, the person responsible for acquisitions should decide.

If everyone within the organization knows and makes fast decisions within the parameters of the same set of guiding principles, the vast majority of the decisions made will be the right ones. Randall Mays, CFO of Clear Channel Communications, says there's no way his company would have become the world's largest out-of-home media company in less than a decade if they had an entrenched bureaucracy making decisions:

> What allowed us to think and move so fast is that, as we expanded, it didn't put pressure on an infrastructure. We didn't have a bureaucracy to put stress on. We have been able to go from 14 to nearly 1,000 radio stations because each is a decentralized, autonomous unit. As we add additional radio stations, we just plug them in.

His brother Mark, the firm's president and COO, says, "Our home office structure has never changed. We refuse to have a big bureaucratic mess for people to fight through. We don't want any red tape getting in the way of our people." Mark then explains:

> Look, we hire the best people and then get out of their way. The worst thing we could do would be to set central policy or micromanage them. The best sales, programming, and promotional decisions are made on the local level. We hire entrepreneurs and let them do their own thinking.

HOW DO YOU GET RID OF THE BUREAUCRACY?

You blow it up as fast as you can! Having been involved in scores of successful turnarounds and hopefully having learned from those that weren't as successful, we maintain that if a company wants to become a faster-thinking and -acting organization, bureaucratic structures need to be destroyed as quickly, fairly, firmly, and efficiently as possible.

In the early 1990s, we were hired to assist in the transformation and financial turnaround of RNZ. This commercial radio network with fifty radio stations across New Zealand was owned by the government, which wanted to make the company look more like a commercial venture prior to its being auctioned off. We had no idea how firmly entrenched a bureaucracy we'd find.

Within the first few hours, we uncovered a central office supply system that required nine forms in order to get a pad of paper, a score of voice coaches (we had guessed radio announcers could already speak), a sign over the urinal advising us to see the company's executive nurse if we noticed any unusual growths because it was National Wart Week, and we were almost run over in the hallway by a uniformed "tea lady" pushing a trolley filled with goodies for the managers.

It didn't surprise us that the company was hemorrhaging money, that no one was empowered to make a decision, and that everyone had the same glare in their eyes as when you catch a deer in the headlights. What did surprise us was that it eventually took six CEOs nearly ten years before a seventh CEO finally made the tough calls, destroyed the bureaucracy, and turned the organization into a nimble, powerful, profitable blowtorch that, as one of our associates who remained with the company says, "now runs on the smell of an oily rag."

Along the way, lives, hopes, dreams, and careers were disrupted and in some cases ended by CEOs too afraid or paralyzed to dismantle the bureaucracy that was slowing them down. Instead of one big cut of the scores of unnecessary bureaucrats in order to restore the organization to health, constant small cuts kept everyone focused on who would be the next casualty and what they should do to protect themselves.

It is as unfair to slowly dismantle a bureaucratic structure as it would be for a surgeon to open up a patient once a year and remove 10 percent of a cancerous tumor. Here is the way it should be done: When Sweden's Percy Barnevik's company ASEA succeeded in making a play for the troubled Swiss giant Brown Boveri, he promptly sent a message to the thousands of bureaucrats who worked at the company's home office in Zurich, Switzerland:

In the future, Barnevik is reputed to have said, the company won't be run like a government and administered from a central home office. Everyone at head office has ninety days to find a real job within the company that has something to do with *touching* a customer.

Gulp. There was the predictable wailing and gnashing of teeth and protest, but ninety days later Barnevik made good on his promise.

More than 3,000 Swiss bureaucrats, unclear on the concept of the customer, found themselves staring at empty muesli bowls when they were unable to comply. The once stodgy company—where decisions took months—quickly transformed itself from a lumbering power transmission and distribution, oil, gas, and petroleum and building technology company into a quick-thinking company where all decisions are made in 1,000 local offices by 170,000 associates and employees.

Predictably, since the departure of the bureaucrats and the end of "central" decision making, the new ASEA Brown Boveri has sizzled, going from one strength to another and currently earning profits in excess of $2.5 billion annually.

USE BARNEVIK'S DICTUM: GET RID OF
90 PERCENT OF THE HOME OFFICE

Barnevik's standard operating procedure for dismantling bureaucratic structures is a simple one: 30 percent of all bureaucrats can be rehabilitated by being sent to an operating unit and made into profitable personnel, 30 percent can be spun off into new profit centers, 30 percent can be eliminated as superfluous, and 10 percent are required to run the home office.

WHO STAYS . . . WHO GOES?

In the fastest companies, executives who have a *direct* involvement with finding, keeping, or growing customers stay. Everyone else is excluded from the operational decision-making process.

Finding means leading the process of acquiring new customers. *Keeping* means leading the process of exceeding the expectations of the customers. *Growing* means creating relevant new products and services to increase customer spending and loyalty.

The only other home office folks—*as opposed to leaders*—required are for accounting (to make certain the numbers are right), tax (to pay as little as legally possible), legal (to stay out of trouble), and human resource (to find, keep, and grow the right people) issues. And, unless a decision calls for their input because of their unique expertise, they should stay in their office, do their job, and not be involved in a decision-making process that doesn't and shouldn't involve them. Although it's become increasingly popular to involve every executive in every decision, the last thing an organization needs to do—*if it wishes to make fast decisions*—is involve people who know nothing about finding, keeping, and growing customers in decisions that involve those core activities.

What does the chief legal counsel know about marketing and why would you want his or her opinion? The current trend to create a sense of inclusion by involving every executive in every decision betrays the leader's ability to make a decision without a consensus. Consensus slows an organization's ability to make speedy decisions.

Alongside strong financial controls, if every executive in a company had to pass the litmus test of being involved in finding, keeping, and growing the right customers, the organization would remain lightning fast in its ability to make fast decisions. In future chapters, you'll learn how to create small autonomous operating units unburdened by bureaucratic B.S.

[A SIXTY-SECOND HEADS-UP] ➡

- Don't B.S. yourself—it'll slow you down.
- Figure out if your organization is or is becoming bureaucratic.
- Dismantle it fast.
- Apply Barnevik's dictum.
- Unless every member of the leadership team has direct involvement and responsibility for finding, keeping, and growing the right customers, the seeds of a bureaucracy have already been sown within the organization.

UNBUNDLE EVERYTHING

When it's your own idea that requires a decision, putting it through the "grinder" should be sufficient. But when someone else comes to you for a decision and it must be made quickly, there's another tactic you should use.

THE CASE OF THE "ORTHODOX" PRIEST

An entrepreneurial brother-and-sister team anticipated that a once shabby neighborhood was on the verge of breaking through and becoming San Francisco's next hot area. (This actual event took place in San Francisco's South of Market area. Fortunately, we were observers, not investors. We've elected not to use real names. Enough people have already been sued.)

Spotting a long vacant building that had housed a printing company—a perfect building for a huge nightclub/entertainment venue—they approached the owner who had listed it for sale. The owner wouldn't give them an option and said that he wanted a fast deal.

The brother and sister quickly hired a prominent local attorney who checked the zoning rules and talked with his cronies at city hall; he couldn't find a reason why the building couldn't become a nightclub, so they mortgaged themselves to the hilt and bought the building.

They quickly put together a group of other investors including the area's premiere nightclub builder, who agreed to do the project, the only caveat being that because he was a little short of cash his investment would have to be the final $500,000 in the $8 million project. He explained to the duo that if he wasn't able to commence work soon, he'd be forced to take other jobs to keep his crews working and might not be available for their project. Assuring them it was safe to start construction before all the permits were granted, he suggested they begin the interior demolition and build out.

"It's done all the time," he promised. All he needed was a check for $250,000 to begin the demolition. Based on the assurances of their legal eagle that such a course of action was routine, the investors coughed up the dough and the contractor began work.

The contractor's advice was apparently sound. Giving the brother, sister, and their attorney a wink, the head of the Building Permits Department assured them the final permits would be issued soon. The interior demolition was then completed and the contractor needed another $400,000 to keep going. Not a problem. After all, the head of the Permits Department had assured them everything was okay.

The investors all saw the vision. They were excited. The $400,000 check and several more for equally large amounts were issued in the next few weeks. Money was being spent at a prodigious rate.

Everyone was caught up in the excitement. Stages, staircases, and bars were starting to take shape . . . it was all happening so fast. One day, a priest from a small Orthodox church a few blocks away stopped by the construction site, was warmly greeted by the contractor's crew, and was proudly shown the project. The next day, he returned with a few other local business owners. They had a few questions.

Fast forward. A grassroots community protest was launched. Public hearings were held. Stop orders were issued.

It seemed you weren't allowed to have a nightclub within 750 feet of a house of worship. It didn't matter that the parish had fewer than twenty members or that the law had never been enforced previously and the area was filled with other clubs.

Community interests prevailed. The verdict came in. There wasn't going to be a nightclub. Huge fines were levied. The investors couldn't or wouldn't pay them. Liens were placed on the building.

Everyone howled, wagged accusatory fingers, and sued everyone else. The brother-and-sister team stopped speaking to one another. They both declared bankruptcy.

Everyone got a bad deal except for the contractor, who pushed for and had received a fast decision. The contractor had presented them a "bundled" proposal: They wanted him to do the work (he'd sold them well), he'd become an investor (big promise—no money), he needed to start soon (the old sense-of-urgency scam), and starting soon wouldn't be a problem (the big titillating promise). He did them in.

BEWARE OF PACKAGE DEALS AND PACKAGE DECISIONS

Package decisions are a lot like the direct mail offers from the telephone companies. Chances are you've seen their offers for bundled plans. "Let us handle all your telecommunication needs," they advertise, "and we'll give it all to you for one great price." But when you carefully examine the component parts, you discover one good deal alongside one or two dead dogs that have been bundled up in the package.

Chances are better than 90 percent that by the time a need for a quick decision reaches your desk, someone has tried to bundle up, hide, or disguise her pet project or protect her self-interests in the proposition. The challenge for those who want to improve their ability to make fast decisions is to perfect the skill of unbundling decision packages and to be able to quickly assess the best and worst scenario for each component.

The fastest and most accurate decision makers have trained themselves and everyone around them to always break the decision down into bite-sized pieces, review each piece, make a series of small judgments, and then make the big decision. The brother and sister in our example did many things right. They spotted a trend and correctly anticipated the neighborhood would become the next hot area. It did. Being unfamiliar with the local area, they hired the best available legal counsel and even turned down a number of prospective investors who didn't quite see their precise vision. Their undoing was in failing to question the role of the contractor's self-interests and unbundling the package he presented to them.

BE AN ESKIMO

We couldn't help but be amused by another guest at a recent party we attended. She was in her late twenties, and although the highlights of her resume were the eight years she had spent trying to finish a four-year degree, having done serious time as a cocktail waitress and selling real estate part-time, she had recently reinvented herself as a budding Internet entrepreneur. We admit she had mastered being disdainful of anything having to do with the old economy and she was pretty good at parroting terms such as *lockout period, universal products, metrics, angels, first round,* and *second round.*

As the evening progressed, we couldn't help but overhear a heated discussion she was having with another guest—an accomplished and revered business tycoon—about how many founder's shares she should demand for her involvement in a new start-up. It was tough keeping a straight face as the guest she had cornered kept trying to get away from her and her nonstop, unintelligible jargon. No one had taught her the lesson of the Eskimo—that smart is dumb and dumb is smart.

In interviewing hundreds of the world's fastest businesspeople for this book, we couldn't help but notice that they all had perfected the art—perhaps without even being aware of it—of playing dumb. People who try to impress you by pretending to be smart generally aren't. Truly smart people know that by playing dumb and asking the other party to repeat or explain things several times, asking lots of questions, they'll be better prepared to respond and then make a fast decision.

When unbundling a decision package, the questions that skilled and fast decision makers always ask are:

- What are the self-interests of the person asking me to make this decision?
- Will their interests be served more than those of the business?
- What are the component parts of the proposition?
- What are the worst and best scenarios for each component?
- Have all the possible consequences of the decision been considered?

A fast decision should not be made until these questions are answered.

[**A SIXTY-SECOND HEADS-UP**]

- Beware of package deals and package propositions.
- Most packaged decisions are filled with hidden agendas.
- Remember the rule of the Eskimo: Smart is dumb and dumb is smart.
- Smart, fast decision makers unbundle every decision they're asked to make.

SHUFFLE PORTFOLIOS

Almost all businesses exhibit the shortsighted tendency of putting people in a position and then keeping them in the same position as long as they perform well. How dumb!

The fastest-thinking companies in the world take an entirely different approach. Anyone who wants to create an environment where decisions are made quickly, correctly, and unemotionally will embrace the tactic of constantly shuffling portfolios. Shuffling portfolios flies in the face of the conventional business wisdom that constantly touts the value of building "relationships," but executives and companies that don't do it are far slower decision makers than their rivals.

When we owned our first radio station, we accidentally stumbled on the concept while trying to prove a point. As an experiment and despite the whining, crying, and threats of the salespeople, we took the account list of salesperson A and assigned it to salesperson B and vice versa. The results were startling.

Within weeks, both lists of clients were far outperforming their previous year's revenue production. We began shuffling some more and discovered the more we shuffled (to a point) the more productive the client lists became. Our shuffling of accounts had inadvertently broken down some of the barriers erected by salespeople that prevent them from achieving the maximum amount of client revenues. These are the same limitations that slow down decision making in businesses that don't shuffle portfolios.

Since that first experiment and as a result of two decades of work with hundreds of companies worldwide, as well as our research into the fastest companies in the world, we've become huge proponents of frequently shuffling portfolios or areas of responsibility.

YOUR ANSWER WILL TELL A LOT
ABOUT THE WAY YOU THINK.

QUESTION

John is a manager of a mutual fund responsible for the deployment of $500 million. Having taken over management of the fund five years previously, which year do you think he turned in his best financial performance?

POSSIBLE ANSWERS

A. Year 1

B. Year 2

C. Year 5

THE CORRECT ANSWER

Most people get it wrong. Dr. Richard Geist is a professor of psychiatry at the Harvard Medical School and author of *Richard Geist's Strategic Investments*. After researching the performance of thousands of mutual funds, Dr. Geist concludes that a fund manager's best year will likely be his or her first. He calls it the "First-year phenomenon." Dr. Geist theorizes that during a fund manager's first year, he or she is without a need to defend the previous year's choices and is able to ruthlessly assess the viability and potential performance of holdings in the fund.

Bruce Ritter is a highly successful investment counselor who has spent years handling and managing the investments of high-net-worth families. When we posed the previous question to him, not only did he get the answer right, without pausing to consider his response, but also added, "The most difficult thing about taking on a new client is to have them sit there and say, 'No, you can't sell this one . . . please,' or, 'I really want to hold on to that one,' and 'Please don't sell that stock . . . it's one of my favorites.' "

Similar to Geist's argument that fund managers should be forced to frequently start over from scratch, Ritter maintains that everyone should be forced to cash in their portfolio once every three years and make all new choices unburdened by the need to defend what they presently own. When a managers or executives sit in the same chair and carry the same responsibilities for longer than eighteen months to two years, they stop making the fast decisions required in today's business environment and invariably slow down.

SEVEN REASONS TO FREQUENTLY SHUFFLE PORTFOLIOS

1. PEOPLE GET ATTACHED

It's human nature. Everyone gets attached and emotionally involved with things they've researched, considered, and chosen. Dr. Geist believes the problem for many managers of mutual funds is that at the end of a reporting period they face a conundrum—they wouldn't buy what's in their portfolio but they won't sell it either due to their need to defend their choices.

When you shuffle portfolios frequently, you're developing business decision makers who make their decisions based only on the facts, unencumbered with the emotional baggage of needing to defend their past choices.

2. TOO MUCH CONFIDENCE GETS PEOPLE IN TROUBLE

In prehistoric times, confidence didn't assure man a better chance of survival, but it did attract mates, allies, and opportunities. Therefore, things worked out better for people who radiated confidence. Those genes prevailed.

The holdover is that today realism is often discounted and overconfidence runs rampant in most business circles. Many people incorrectly believe that all you need is the right attitude to make the most of every situation.

Lowell Busenitz and Jay Barney, professors of management at the University of Houston, studied 124 entrepreneurs and 95 managers. Their conclusion was that entrepreneurs were much more confident about their answers to questions about business and current events . . . *especially when they were wrong.* Confidence leads people to opportunism (a good thing) and delusion (not so good). When you shuffle portfolios, people have neither the time nor the luxury to become overconfident.

3. PEOPLE SLACK OFF . . . WHEN THEY GET THE BUSINESS

Remember the great credit-card offer you received? No interest for the first six months, the bank claimed, and they made a guaranteed, promised, written-in-blood oath that your rate would never be higher than 6.5 percent. When you dialed the special "customer care" number for prospective cardholders your call was answered on the first ring by someone whose friendliness was unmatched. You signed up.

Six months later, when you casually glanced at your monthly statement and were shocked to see you were being charged 19.5 percent interest, you called again. It took scores of rings and an endless wait on hold before someone finally came on the line. You found yourself trying to communicate with an unfriendly, argumentative, unintelligible, uncaring nincompoop.

Or, what about the supplier who worked so furiously to impress you and get your business? For a few months, things were fine, then the original sales rep left, the stable prices you'd been promised began increasing with alarming frequency, and your calls for help were met with a deafening silence.

Most people would keep the credit card and the supplier. It's just too hard to change. Companies, vendors, and suppliers know people abhor change.

A new person with a fresh perspective is willing to correct

defects immediately. When the responsibilities of managers and executives are frequently shifted, relationships with vendors, suppliers, and customers—*all the people who can potentially do you in*—remain under constant scrutiny and review. Those who no longer deliver as agreed are replaced.

4. SAVE THE GOLDEN MEMORIES FOR A FIFTIETH WEDDING ANNIVERSARY

We all have a tendency to remember the good and forget the bad, recall the pleasure and forget the pain. A new decision maker isn't hindered by memories. When someone new is placed in charge, the short-term payoff will likely be higher productivity. The long-term payoff will be someone who makes fast decisions, unencumbered with nice memories. His or her only interest will be in having everyone perform as agreed.

Because of their lightning-fast growth, Charles Schwab has institutionalized the shuffling of portfolios and requires that job applicants be capable of doing the job of someone three ranks above them. In a typical year, Schwab staff members and supervisors will report to as many as three different bosses.

5. THE LAW OF REVERSION TO THE MEANS WON'T APPLY . . . AS SOON

Reversion to the means says, "The physical product (your profits) of any factor of products (your business) will decline at some point." (This is our simplified explanation based on complex definitions in various standard economic dictionaries.) In other words, whoever is number one eventually won't be—the top dog is always unseated.

Doing the same thing, the same way, with the same people in place, will result in the law of reversion to the means catching up with you faster. The law of reversion to the means applies to every business, but constantly changing portfolios ensures the business of a nonstop stream of new ideas gained through constantly changing perspectives that will defer it.

6. SHUFFLING PORTFOLIOS MAKES TURTLE SOUP SENSE

An old Chinese proverb says, "If you find a turtle on a pole, someone put it there." Whether it's a bagel shop in Manhattan or a multinational corporation with hundreds of worldwide facilities, most companies are filled with turtles sitting atop poles. Some bugger put them there and they slow everything down, especially the making of fast decisions.

You probably know these turtles better by their lunchroom names. There's the *Harpy*, who bottlenecks human resources, and *Admiral Dipshit*, who has a lock on the best sales territory and couldn't close his own zipper. There's *Old Yellow Stain*, the supervisor who has been circling the drain for years but still shows up to slow down every decision, the *Buttboys*, who question everything but offer no solutions, and the *Fashion Victims* from advertising.

As long as the same managers are kept in the same positions making the same decisions, all the turtles get to stay perched atop their poles doing nothing but slowing everything down. When you frequently shuffle portfolios, the turtles get discovered, knocked off their poles, and turned into turtle soup.

7. SHUFFLING PORTFOLIOS KEEPS EVERYONE ON THEIR TOES

Occasionally, following a lecture on the shuffling of portfolios, we're challenged by someone offering what he or she believes is a "gottcha" question: "Should everyone's portfolio be shuffled, even doctors and pilots?" We answer by pointing out that the Mayo Clinic is constantly rated the number one hospital in the nation (if not the world) and that most of the hundreds of thousands of patients who visit it each year have been referred by regular family doctors who want another physician to check things out, in essence *shuffling their own portfolio*. And, commercial pilots hardly fly the same craft each day and are deliberately kept on their toes by the required completion of a preflight checklist prior to takeoff.

The biggest benefit derived from frequently shuffling portfolios is that it keeps everyone just a little off guard, constantly striving to do their best and to exceed expectations. The alternative is a comfortable, settled environment that doesn't welcome or adapt well to change, where decisions are made ponderously. By constantly shuffling portfolios, patients, and airplanes, everyone is kept on their toes . . . exactly where you want them to be.

[**A SIXTY-SECOND HEADS-UP**] ➡

- In the first-year phenomenon, individuals don't need to defend their past decisions, are willing to make tough calls, and can get rid of the dogs and move on.
- The seven reasons to frequently shuffle portfolios:

  I. People get emotionally attached to their decisions.

2. Business people have to defend their wrong decisions more arduously than their correct ones. Too much confidence can get them into trouble.

3. Vendors, suppliers, and customers tend to slack off after the honeymoon. The constant scrutiny provided by a new decision maker keeps everyone dancing.

4. Decision makers tend to remember the good and forget the bad—all the more reason to constantly change portfolios.

5. It ensures a nonstop source of new ideas.

6. It helps unmask the sacred cows.

7. It keeps everyone on their toes.

CONSTANTLY REASSESS EVERYTHING

*U*nless a company constantly reassesses every decision it makes and every direction it takes, it will eventually end up as road kill. Perhaps there was an easier, gentler time when challenges were familiar and management's job was demanding but not particularly creative. Managers counted stuff, allocated assets, and solved occasional problems. Constant reassessment wasn't required.

Then, in the 1980s, revolutionary technologies, consolidation, well-funded new competition, unpredictable consumers, and a quickening in the pace of change hurled unfamiliar conditions at management. How did that crop of managers do?

According to consultant and author Gary Hamel, "Between 1985 and 1995, fewer than forty companies of the Fortune 1,000 grew total shareholder returns by more than 25 percent annually." That is, 96 percent of the Fortune 1,000 proved themselves incapable of moving fast enough to keep pace with what was happening on the outside.

Adjusted for inflation, the annual growth rate of the S&P 500 averaged a dismal 1.4 percent between 1984 and 1994.

According to Hamel's research, the forty companies that did experience significant growth didn't achieve it through cost cutting, stock repurchase, megamergers, or any conventional asset manipulation. "Instead," Hamel argues, "these fast companies averaged compounded annual *revenue* gains of 25.3 percent during the time frame." Hamel concluded his research by noting that these forty companies either invented totally new industries or radically changed existing ones.

Companies can only invent new businesses or drastically alter existing ones when they're prepared to constantly reassess every past decision. Every business—including yours—has a giant *use-by date* stamped on its back just like a carton of milk. Everything that exists is getting old, wearing out, and will be replaced.

Jack Welch of General Electric does a good job of illustrating the need for constant reassessment when he says, "If the rate of change inside an organization is less than the rate of change outside . . . their end is in sight." One of the tools used by Welch to ensure constant reassessment is the annual review undertaken by every GE executive and staff member. Once a year, everyone's performance is evaluated and awarded a numerical ranking of between 1 and 5. The implicit understanding is that both the individual and his or her score are moving up or it's time to leave the company.

Home Depot, GE, Dell, and The Gap are highly successful examples of companies that prospered between 1985 and 1995 by constantly reassessing every decision they made and quickly changing direction as required. Following them in the 1990s and into the new millennium are AOL, Charles Schwab, Lend Lease, H&M, Clear Channel, Telepizza, and others whose stories are told in this book.

DARWIN HAD IT RIGHT

When famed anthropologist Charles Darwin concluded that, "It's not the strongest nor most intelligent of the species that survive; it is the one most adaptable to change," he could have been writing about the life expectancies of business. For years, Intel refused to build and sell processors for the sub–$1,000 PC market. Intel's chairperson, Andy Grove, even had a label for it: Segment Zero. But between 1994 and 1998, Grove watched as Segment Zero grew 400 percent to represent one out of every five computers sold. Andy Grove shook off his preconceptions about maintaining margin and immediately put 650 engineers to work. They recased every budget and created Celeron, the Intel processor for the sub–$1,000 market. Intel *reassessed* and adapted.

Charles Schwab founded a discount brokerage business and the word *advice* was forbidden. It was a firing offense. He frequently said, "If we're going to be the most ethical and useful brokerage house in the world, advice is something we'll never give." But as more and more customers asked for help, Schwab *reassessed* and adapted. During a late-night drive in 1995 through southern California, he turned to Dave Pottruck and said, "We're going to have to become more involved in our customers' outcomes." In the next three years, Schwab grew 70 percent, as advice quickly became the biggest part of their business.

When he founded Hotmail, Sabeer Bhatia was leading the company down three separate tracks. In *reassessing* that decision, Bhatia chose to concentrate on one area—free e-mail for consumers—where his company could cause a revolution. Another company could have beaten Hotmail had Bhatia failed to constantly reassess.

Lend Lease is among a handful of companies that can claim to have grown shareholder value 25 percent annually for more than twenty-five years. Stuart Hornery, who has led the company for more than two decades, credits the firm's ability to move quickly to their willingness to annually *reassess* everything they do, including the businesses they own, every decision that is made, and the validity of all executive positions.

MOST PEOPLE HATE REASSESSING BECAUSE OF . . .

- The trap of incumbency
- The belief that if it's not broke, don't even look at it
- Not wanting to confront failure
- Laziness

THE TRAGEDY OF INCUMBENCY

Tragedy is about the inevitable fall of the once great. History proves that tragically all incumbents come to believe they're omnipotent and take their success for granted.

Consider success in business. An entrepreneur puts together a unique and valuable combination of strategy, capabilities, relationships, and processes. The enterprise stands above the crowd. As their recipe succeeds, customers multiply, talent rushes to climb on board, investors bid up the value, and a crowd of competitors starts to imitate. This is seen as positive feedback by managers and owners, and it gives them confidence. They begin to believe they've found the one true path.

Eventually, values become dogma, focus turns into shortsightedness, relationships become shackles, and processes become unquestioned routines. All energies are focused on refining the "winning" formula.

Many books have been written (including one by the boss himself) purporting to explain why Michael Dell was able to found a company in his university dorm room that, within a decade, had a larger market capitalization than Hewlett Packard and Compaq and was within spitting distance of IBM. (May 2000 market capitalization : Dell 132 billion, HP 127 billion, Compaq 47 billion, IBM 179 billion.) We think the way Michael Dell ate everyone's lunch illustrates the point. In addition to correctly anticipating and spotting trends (see Part I), he wasn't burdened by the tragedy of incumbency. He didn't have the blinders, shackles, or dogma of the computer-selling elite. He reassessed everything to which the company was devoted. Meanwhile, IBM, DEC, HP, and legions of other technology companies went about business as usual and dismissed Dell's efforts. Today, they're all rushing to imitate Michael Dell's success.

Most company executives incorrectly think their efforts and resources should be spent "perfecting" their current business model rather than constantly reassessing it. Most incumbent market leaders become burdened by huge infrastructure, giant bureaucracies, overheads, ego, delusion, and process counting. Their unwillingness and inability to reassess everything eventually catches up with them. If you close your eyes and listen carefully, you can almost hear the ghosts of businesses past sitting in plush cobweb-strewn offices and mahogany boardrooms coughing up their wisdom:

"We know our competitors inside out."

Could Kmart or Levitz Furniture have said it?

"We're not the world's greatest innovator, but we run a tight ship."

Doesn't it sound like Sears or Marks and Spencer?

"If it ain't broke, we don't fix it."

You can almost hear the echo of Encyclopedia Britannica.

"We can allow ourselves to become distracted by all the new fads in the marketplace."

Can't you imagine hearing a Merrill Lynch executive mouthing these words?

"We don't want to alienate the partners within our current distribution system."

We wonder if someone at Firestone made that statement.

"We have a world-class, stable management team."

Whatever happened to Digital Equipment Corporation?

The primary challenge facing market leaders is to institutionalize an environment where every decision and direction can be constantly and safely reassessed.

IF IT AIN'T BROKE . . .

Conventional wisdom says, "If it ain't broke, don't fix it." In the mid-1990s, management guru and author Tom Peters began proclaiming, "If it ain't broke, break it!" Unfortunately, for the long-term success of their shareholders and increasingly their own tenure, most suits quietly believe and practice another superstitious variant: "If it ain't broke, don't even look at it. You might spook it."

The same person or team responsible for the success of an enterprise becomes the company's worst enemy when they fail to constantly reassess decisions and direction.

DEALING WITH FAILURE ISN'T FUN

It's almost as if when Buddha said, "Success has a hundred parents, but failure is an orphan," he was talking about business in the twenty-first century. When a business introduces a new product or service and hits a home run, everyone involved—no matter how marginal their contribution—clamors to hop aboard the handshake and bonus express. But when an initiative fails, everyone casts their eyes toward the floor in hopes of not being seen as having played even a minor role. Consider the six phases in the life of new initiatives:

- Wild enthusiasm

- Disillusionment

- Total confusion

- Search for the guilty

- Punishment of the innocent

- Promotion of the nonparticipants

Business has traditionally done an abysmal job of dealing with failure. If a new initiative is a huge flop, a sacrificial lamb may be offered up for slaughter, a few other people may be reassigned, and the entire sordid mess is never discussed again. It's almost as though people are fearful that failure is catchy.

Because few people enjoy dealing with failure, most companies brush their failed initiatives aside, the person in charge makes some silly speech filled with war talk about charging ahead, and the company learns nothing from the experience. One result of this institutionalized aversion to failure is that companies are fearful of reassessing. They might have to confront their mistakes.

Firestone was one of the most dominant and well-known tire brands in the world, but their refusal to reassess decisions brought them to their knees. As their sales tumbled, so did manufacturing. Eventually, the company was only able to keep their factories working at 50 percent of capacity and they were gobbled up by an upstart—Bridgestone—for pennies on the dollar. Firestone's unwillingness to reassess caused them to miss . . . the radial tire.

LAZINESS

With the achievement of any objective comes the urge to rejoice and relax. A typical human fault is that upon achieving a goal people resist the call to get going and do it all over again. When organizations become lazy, reassessment of every action is the first thing to be dropped. Sloppy decisions invariably follow.

When famous jazz violinist Stefan Grapelli was asked why, after sixty years as a successful musician, he didn't take a break, he replied that he frequently had the urge but was afraid, saying, "If I ever stopped, I might not get started again." One big difference we've noted in studying fast companies is that while they briefly pause to celebrate victories, so strong is the company's crusade (see Part III) that the next day everyone's back in the saddle eager and ready to face the next set of hurdles, even if it means undoing the very thing that provided them the previous day's win.

FOUR STEPS FOR REASSESSMENT

When a company decides to embrace the concept of ongoing reassessment, it would be wise to borrow the four tactics employed by the world's fastest companies.

1. CREATE AN ENVIRONMENT WHERE NOBLE FAILURES ARE CELEBRATED

Dave Pottruck, the CEO of Schwab, says, "The idea that failure is okay is ridiculous. I am not going to go around the company and reward someone for failing. But here at Schwab we differentiate between *noble* failure and *stupid* failure." Pottruck says that Charles Schwab has a set of criteria for defining noble failure:

> Noble failures occur when you have a good plan and know what you're doing, you've thought everything through carefully, and have implemented with sufficient management discipline, that if you looked back in review, you'd conclude it was thoughtfully done.
>
> Then there must be a reasonable contingency plan to deal with any initial failure and the contingency plan must have been implemented.
>
> Finally, you need to debrief yourself and ask what you can learn from the experience that will lead us as a company to be smarter next time. When each of those criteria has been met, then a failure can be described as being *noble*.

Schwab journals their failures and lessons they've learned, maintains a museum-like display of failed innovations, and even created a videotape for employee orientation, hosted by Pottruck and Charles Schwab, chronicling their failures. How many other CEOs do you think would agree to host such a video?

When the celebration of noble failure becomes institutionalized, people within the organization are more willing to reassess earlier decisions.

2. GIVE EVERYONE WITHIN THE ORGANIZATION AN ANNUAL NUMERICAL RANKING

Once a year, everyone within an organization should receive a numerical ranking between 1 and 5.

5 = EXCEPTIONAL	You created extraordinary value, handled new responsibilities flawlessly, and launched successful new initiatives.
4 = VERY GOOD	You created discernible value and either handled new responsibilities well or were responsible for successful new initiatives.
3 = AVERAGE	You're a solid team player.
2 = BELOW AVERAGE	You might have one year to fix things, but you're in the departure lounge.
1 = FAILING	You are out of here. Who hired you? Why did your managers allow it to get this far?

By reassessing every staff member annually, an organization creates a culture that will be more prepared to reassess everything frequently.

3. HOLD AN ANNUAL REASSESSMENT RETREAT

The top executives at Lend Lease all agree on one thing: the annual reassessment exercise chaired by Stuart Hornery during the firm's early years is largely responsible for the firm's stellar success. Once each year, Hornery gathered the key executives of the company in a room filled with white boards and large pads of paper. No one—including Hornery—was certain where the exercise would end up. Everything was up for discussion including job titles, responsibilities, assignments, what businesses the company would be involved in, other corporations they might purchase, and world-class projects in which they wanted to become involved.

During the Lend Lease retreats, every previous decision and assumption was challenged. By the end of the session, people often found themselves with brand-new jobs, compensation packages, and responsibilities, often in charge of an operating unit with which they had never been involved. When businesses—notwithstanding their size—commit to an annual reassessment of everything, they've unwittingly created a culture of *constant* reassessment.

4. ASSIGN TEAMS TO REASSESS

There are a number of risks inherent in having individuals perform the job of reassessing:

- They are limited by their perspective or view of the world.

- They may be personally invested in the project they're being asked to assess.

- Nobody wants to be seen as a killjoy.

- There are political dangers inherent in reassessing an initiative conceived or sponsored by someone else. Nobody enjoys making enemies.

Whether you own a restaurant, a one-person financial services firm, or a giant company with tens of thousands of employees, it's better to call on the collective talents of a small team to quickly reassess past decisions and directions.

[A SIXTY-SECOND HEADS-UP]

- The financial performance of companies that invent new businesses or radically alter existing models is far superior to those that don't.
- Inventing new businesses and/or dramatically altering existing models requires constant reassessment.
- Most people are reluctant to constantly reassess because of:

   The trap of incumbency

   A reluctance to examine what isn't broken

   An institutionalized aversion to failure

   Laziness

- There are four steps for institutionalizing constant reassessment:

   Celebrate noble failures.

   Reassess everyone within the company annually.

   Hold an annual reassessment retreat.

   Assign reassessment teams.

PART III

GET TO MARKET FASTER

A senior telecom executive was recently quoted as saying, "Show me someone with a five-year plan and I'll show you someone who has no idea of what's going on." We agree.

The game is about speed—getting to market in weeks or months, not years, and doing it faster than anyone else. Once we identified the fastest companies in the world, we went inside them, hung out with and studied the people who made/make it happen, and discovered the things they do to prevent speed bumps from slowing them down. This section explains the tactics used by the fastest companies to create new services and products and get them to market faster than anyone else:

- LAUNCH A CRUSADE.

- OWN AND EXPLOIT YOUR COMPETITIVE ADVANTAGE.

- GET VENDORS AND SUPPLIERS TO MOVE FAST.

- STAY BENEATH THE RADAR.

- KEEP IT SIMPLE.

- INSTITUTIONALIZE INNOVATION.

- GET OTHER FAST PEOPLE ON YOUR SIDE.

LAUNCH A CRUSADE

The fastest companies in the world—those that get to market fastest—don't waste time sitting around a conference table processing visions with the creative types from HR. They don't need to. They share something bigger and stronger. Each has a *cause* that they use to launch *crusades*.

A CRUSADE IS THE STARTING POINT
FOR FAST AND FIRST TO MARKET

Whether it's a restaurant with 15 employees or a software firm with 10,000, most companies are filled with people who have no clue of the big picture—what the organization is really trying to accomplish—and because they don't feel that they or their contributions are important, they do their job . . . and nothing more. How much faster would your business be able to bring new products/services to market if everyone within the organization had their heart and soul wrapped up in taking aim and shooting at the same target?

In less than a year, Charles Schwab took e.schwab from an idea to market to runaway success. According to Dave Pottruck, "Everyone at the company is part of our crusade or they don't last long."

People joined Sabeer Bhatia to build something that had never been built in return for zero salary or benefits—only the promise of a small piece of the company if and when a payday ever came. Together, within a matter of months, they took Hotmail from an idea to a product that brought the company millions of clients. The people who went to work for Bhatia didn't join a company; they joined a crusade.

When desirable locations become available, H&M can look at the property, cut a deal, and be open for business within weeks. Everyone who works for and contracts H&M becomes part of their crusade.

Compare the way H&M, Hotmail, and Schwab get to market fast with Hewlett Packard, where a top executive who recently jumped ship to spin-off Agilent confessed to us recently that it takes a minimum of two years to deliver a new product to market at HP. "None of that time is for think time," he lamented further. "The two years are from the time the idea is done." When asked why it took so long, his reply was terse: "There's too many speed bumps in the way, too many damn engineers who only see things their way, and too many processes and structures to cut through. Everyone at HP is always on a different page."

YOU CAN'T LAUNCH A CRUSADE WITHOUT A CAUSE

A cause is the real reason the business exists. A cause answers the big "*Why* am I really doing this?" Contrast the definition of *Cause* with *Vision*.

> **Cause:** *that which gives rise to an action, a motive, a principle, a belief or purpose*

> **Vision:** *something perceived in a dream, trance, spell, or stupor; something supernaturally revealed to a prophet.*

Charles Schwab's cause is: "To be the most ethical and useful financial services company in the world." AOL's cause is: "To build a global medium as central to people's lives as the telephone or television, only more useful." The Hotmail crusade was: "To revolutionize and democratize communications." Clear Channel's crusade is: "Creating value for the shareholder." The Telepizza crusade was: "Creating a world of Telepizza citizens."

WHERE DO CAUSES COME FROM?

Unlike missions and visions, which are generally created by committees and sufficiently watered down to please everyone, offend nobody, and motivate no one, a cause comes from a defining moment in the leader's life.

Charles Schwab worked for other brokerage companies and had witnessed firsthand the disdain that most financial services firms have for their clients and the poor service they give them. Instead of becoming cynical, he felt called to build an "anti-model."

Steve Case had a lackluster college career, did a stint in women's hair care products, and briefly worked for Pizza Hut developing pizza toppings. He was searching for meaning in life and needed to be part of something big and bold.

Sabeer Bhatia wanted to be as rich as many others he saw around him in Silicon Valley. But, had he asked people to join him for zero compensation so that he could become dazzlingly rich, they would have turned him down. Asking people to join him in democratizing communications and changing the world was an easy sell.

Perhaps Lowry Mays's reason for existence—the shareholder—isn't for everyone, but it works for those who have joined him.

Leo Pujals believed Johnson & Johnson treated him unfairly when they failed to keep promises to promote him. At age forty, Pujals risked his life savings in order to build a better company than the one he'd left. As others joined him, he showed them how to achieve financial independence and become what he calls Telepizza citizens.

A cause provides a feeling of belonging, a sense of purpose and loyalty, peer pressure to perform, and a catalyst for action. Dave Pottruck of Schwab says, "People will work hard for money but will give their life for meaning."

THE CRITERIA FOR A CAUSE

Even a crackpot cause will attract followers. But in our study we found eight criteria that were common to the causes of companies that consistently demonstrated an ability to get to market faster than their rivals.

CAUSES ARE NEVER GOALS

Goals can be achieved. Then what? Putting a man on the moon was a goal that enthralled Americans for a decade. When it finally happened, the enthusiasm waned and the space program never regained momentum.

CAUSES BIG ENOUGH FOR CRUSADES COME FROM THE HEART

A cause comes from the heart, not the mind. As we've known since the ancient Greeks, *Homo emotus* (emotional man) is whom we must appeal to if we want to move an organization from *what is* toward *what we want*.

THE BEST CAUSES ARE BIG, BOLD, AND ASPIRATIONAL

No one worth having can get aboard a small cause and crusade. In the early days, Bill Gates's dream of putting a Microsoft Operating System on every desk in the world might have seemed incredulous to some, but it attracted the kind of talent who wanted to move fast.

CAUSES ARE INCLUSIVE

A cause worthy of becoming a crusade speaks to and includes everyone in the organization, not just the bigwigs in the corner office. When Phil Knight, the founder of Nike, says the reason for the existence of his company is "the thrill of competing, winning, and crushing competitors," he's extending an invitation to similarly motivated people to join him and urging those who don't share his view of the world to stay away.

CAUSES AREN'T JUST ABOUT PROFIT

A lot of people are unable to relate to profit. If you doubt this, create as a cause your desire to put fifty cents of every dollar to the bottom line and watch how many people will actively work to see that it isn't achieved. But a cause can be about creating value, as Clear Channel Communications has proven.

An average Clear Channel Communications radio or television station puts between forty and seventy cents of each dollar of revenue to the bottom line. By comparison to most other businesses, this amount is inordinately high. If the Mays family were to parade around their company proclaiming their reason for existence was seventy cents of each dollar to the bottom line, predictably there would be many employees working to see that it didn't happen. But when couched in terms that people can understand—*existing to reward our shareholders for believing and taking a chance on us*—the cause speaks to the heart and the fairness of the reason for existence.

Terry Pearce, author of *Leading Out Loud*, serves as a Schwab fellow and senior vice president. He hardly seems the type to go crazy over someone else's vision. But when he talks about the Schwab cause, he becomes thoughtful, quiet, and misty-eyed:

Look at the difference between working here and someplace else. Here, people are asked to spend their days looking for ways to serve people better and come up with services and products that really make a difference in people's lives. Compare that to being asked to sit around, coming up with a way to make a million dollars. There's no comparison.

BIG CAUSES HAVE AN AHA! EFFECT

In his book *The Age of Unreason*, Charles Handy talks about the need for a cause that ignites people to have an *aha* effect. People hear the words and say, "Aha, but of course, I get that." Any cause that requires lengthy explanation isn't a cause around which a crusade can be built.

A CAUSE NEEDN'T BE CREDIBLE TO THE OUTSIDE WORLD

A cause needs to be believed by the people inside the organization. It doesn't matter how much credibility it has to the outside world or those outside the cause community.

CAUSES ARE EXPRESSED IN FEW WORDS

Walt Disney's cause was building a place to "make people happy." Sam Walton's was to build stores where "the common person could buy the same stuff as rich people." Mary Kay's cause was about creating a company with "unlimited potential for women." Is it only coincidence that these companies also excelled at being fast to market? We don't think so.

TURNING A CAUSE INTO A CRUSADE

One of the chief reasons for the failure of missions and visions to achieve the desired objective is the naiveté of most company managers and executives. Nothing happens by magic. That words on a plaque hanging on the wall or printed on the inside cover of the annual report will change behavior is ludicrous.

Discovering/creating a cause and turning it into a crusade is a replicable model, but it's much more challenging than hanging a sign on the wall. Here are the eight steps we uncovered when examining the histories of companies that use crusades to help them be fast to market.

1. THE LEADER/FOUNDER/CEO MUST LIVE THE CAUSE

Another pearl of wisdom from Charles Handy in *The Age of Unreason* is his statement, "It tempts credulity to proclaim a campaign for the homeless from a penthouse apartment." Before leaders wish to launch a crusade, they must first live the principles associated with the cause. The leader who espouses the value of the customer is exposed as a liar when he or she belittles or takes advantage of one. The manager who talks about speed to market but is playing the process game is quickly exposed as a fraud.

2. THOSE AROUND THE LEADER MUST ALSO LIVE THE CAUSE

If the cause is for real—and not just another tactic to beat more production out of people—leaders will surround themselves with similarly valued and likeminded people who are equally committed to turning the cause into a crusade. But when the leader/manager is seen as indulging someone who isn't on board, or is constantly making exceptions and offering apologies or explanations for another executive's performance, the crusade won't occur.

Kate Rohrbach serves as Schwab's senior VP and chief communication officer. She says that, while the words that describe the Schwab cause and crusade are simple ones, the magic is in seeing them come alive. "It's the authenticity of walking into every single meeting and hearing those words expressed and having them serve as the subtext for every single business decision that's made. That's why I'm here. A cause is personally powerful, sustaining, and rewarding when it's authentic."

3. ALL KEY EXECUTIVES AND MANAGERS MUST *BE SEEN* AS LIVING THE CAUSE

It isn't sufficient for the leadership to live the cause and lead the crusade. It's human nature to look for the bad or the underbelly in someone and not notice the positive. (Managers have done it for centuries—turnabout is fair play.) The executives in charge must go out of their way to *be seen* as living the cause and adhering to the guiding principles of the crusade.

Recently, we saw a high-profile CEO, who happened to be in the middle of a huge cost-cutting crusade, board an airplane for an international flight in a first-class seat. He was unaware—until he received an anonymous note—that way back in the rear of the cattle car sat more than a dozen company staffers who'd recently lost their ability to fly business class.

4. EVERYONE IS INVITED
TO JOIN THE CRUSADE

When the leadership is convinced they're living the cause and there are no visible chinks in their armor, they're ready to launch a crusade. Membership is by invitation only, one at a time, with a brief sit-down meeting explaining the cause, the crusade, the benefits of membership, and an invitation to join. Any company, regardless of employee count, can arrange for private meetings between staff members and their manager or supervisor within a ninety-day time frame.

Everyone is invited. Sometimes hardened cynics who have been disappointed by too many management initiatives will decline. Those are the breaks. Sometimes staff members will be overcome with emotion and perform a Lazarus-rising-from-the-grave number.

One newspaper publisher, in the process of conducting more than 500 private meetings over a three-month period, recounted for us his meeting with a press foreman who had worked tirelessly to thwart every management-sponsored change program for more than twenty years. The newspaper executive told us the surly man strode into his office and thumped himself down into a chair, loudly demanding to know, "What's this bullshit all about?"

By the end of the meeting, fifteen minutes later, he was tearfully explaining that in more than two decades at the paper no executive had ever said hello, much less welcomed him into their office and pledged an end to labor strife—all received for the price of an invitation to join a crusade.

5. THOSE NOT JOINING THE CRUSADE
ARE INVITED TO LEAVE

It's tough to fire people today, and legions of bloodthirsty attorneys will make it tougher in the future. However, when you sit down with someone who has repeatedly been invited to join the crusade and your efforts have been constantly rebuffed, it's time for a final meeting for you to review your previous invitations, extend a final invite, make certain the staff member understands the company won't be abandoning its cause and crusade to mollify him or her, and end the meeting with two questions:

1. Isn't it personally painful to work in a company that is clearly headed in one direction while you are intent on rejecting its reason for existence, guiding principles, and the direction in which it's moving?

2. Wouldn't you be much happier in another environment where you were able to enthusiastically move in the same direction as the rest of the company?

If the employee still refuses to get on board and doesn't decide to leave, either start a file, quickly fill it with three formal warnings, and get this person out the door, or abandon your hopes to lead a crusade.

6. REWARD ACTIVITIES THAT ADVANCE THE CRUSADE
AND PUNISH THOSE THAT DON'T

Most companies make it SOP to reward the wrong activities. The company proclaims one set of values and then bestows big bonuses on a sales, plant, or production manager who gets the business done by lying, deceit, and conduct verging on the illegal. (Do Archer Daniels Midland or American Airlines price-fixing convictions come to mind?) If a company proclaims a cause and launches a crusade, it must be prepared to reward activities that advance the crusade and punish those that don't.

7. CONSTANTLY CELEBRATE THE CAUSE AND CRUSADE

Various research studies have estimated that the typical consumer is bombarded with nearly 3,000 advertising impressions daily. That's a lot of competition for any company wanting to communicate a message to its workers to confront. Unless the Crusade is constantly talked about, reaffirmed, and celebrated, it won't maintain momentum.

Lowry, Mark, and Randall Mays of Clear Channel Communications invoke their commitment to the shareholder hundreds of times daily.

At Hotmail, Sabeer Bhatia was called the "Preacher Man," a title he wore proudly. "Look, he says, the only tool I had was my cause. All I did was walk around the company talking about the grandness of what we were doing and how big and important we would all become." Bhatia argues that business leaders must spend a substantial amount of their time talking about and celebrating the crusade:

> You must evangelize to the people who work for you, to your
> investors, and to your customers. You must constantly communi-
> cate your cause, your enthusiasm and excitement. If you want to

grow a company quickly and get to market fast, you must spend half your time evangelizing and the other half actually managing day-to-day tasks.

8. EVENTUALLY, THE CAUSE AND CRUSADE BECOME THE REASON FOR EXISTENCE

When the previous seven steps are followed, the crusade, the need for speed, and fast to market become a way of life for the organization. On a number of occasions at Schwab, H&M, Clear Channel, Hotmail, and Telepizza, when we asked, "What keeps this crusade going?" the question was met with a wink and a smile, "Everybody says it must be in the water here."

[**A SIXTY-SECOND HEADS-UP**]

- A crusade trumps vision when leading any human organization.
- A crusade requires a cause. It is the real reason for existence.
- Causes
  - Are never goals
  - Are emotional, big, bold, and aspirational
  - Are inclusive
  - Aren't about money or profit
  - Have an Aha! effect
  - Needn't be credible to the outside world
  - Are expressed in only a few words

- Launching a crusade requires
  - The leader must live it
  - All executives and managers must be on board
  - All executives and managers must be seen living it
  - An invitation for everyone to join
  - Those not joining to leave
  - Rewards for conduct that advances the cause
  - That it be constantly celebrated and evangelized

OWN AND EXPLOIT YOUR COMPETITIVE ADVANTAGE

A NEW SOP MIGHT MEAN BEING SOL

The new standard operating procedure screams, "Cut, slash, burn, get rid of everything that isn't vital to the core business." When an outside vendor can do a job more efficiently and cost-effectively than performing the task in-house, outsourcing can make good sense. However, many companies, acting solely in the interest of short-term expense reduction, have tossed the baby out with the bathwater and ended up outsourcing the only thing(s) that allowed them to get to market fast or first. Then they're SOL—shit out of luck!

Companies that are fastest to market have figured out—some consciously and a few accidentally—the importance of owning their competitive advantages. Every business has one or several they can own—the difficulty is in figuring out what they are.

HOW CHARLES SCHWAB ALWAYS
GETS TO MARKET FIRST

When Chuck Schwab launched his discount stock brokerage company, financial services firms routinely outsourced their back-office information technology to other companies. These other companies actually executed the trades, sent written confirmations, prepared monthly client statements, and performed other services requiring mainframe computers.

By 1979, Schwab realized that if he was going to quickly grow the company and gain a competitive advantage, he had to "own" the technology. That same year, he jumped in feet first and purchased a back-office computer system called the Beta System. The price tag was $500,000 and represented a big bet. At the time, the net worth of the entire company was only $500,000. Schwab says that when he signed the contract he was so nervous that his hands were shaking.

Chuck Schwab argues vehemently that you'll never lead in innovation or be faster to market than your competition if you depend on others for your technology. Today, Schwab sees itself as a technology company that just happens to be in the financial services business.

The hardware Schwab purchased required software, which in turn required people to create the software. Soon Schwab possessed a highly skilled in-house technology team. Schwab charged his new team with the admonition, "Create products and services that will serve customers without regard for what can't be done. Push every known boundary."

Given their in-house computing capabilities, Schwab's team quickly began creating one product after another—some were clunkers and others were big successes. Owning the technology—their competitive advantage—provided Schwab the ability to:

- Constantly ask the "what if we could do this" question

- Have the technology ready by the time people knew they wanted it (see Part I)

- Be faster than any other financial service rival in getting to market

In 1982, Schwab introduced the Pocketerm that transmitted stock quotes over an FM receiver. By 1985, they'd released the Equalizer, an umbilical cord between their computers and the customer's computer (consider how few customers had computers in 1985). By 1986, Schwab introduced Schwabline, a portable desktop terminal that transmitted stock quotes over telephone lines and printed them out on adding machine paper.

One after another, the innovations were unleashed on the market. Finally, in 1996, they introduced e.schwab, and the rest is history. They expected 25,000 customers the first year and had more than that number within one month. Within three years, Schwab was handling one of four stock trades in the United States, was receiving nearly 80 million daily hits on their Web site, had opened more than 3 million online accounts, and was worth more than Merrill Lynch.

Owning the technology—Schwab's competitive advantage—is so important to Chuck Schwab that as a further demonstration of his commitment to technology he named Dawn Lepore, the firm's CTO, to the position of vice chair.

HENNES
AND MAURITZ

H&M is the biggest fashion success story of the past decade. They're also the fastest-to-market fashion retailer in the world. Company revenues have doubled every five years like clockwork. Profits increase 22 percent every year (at least they have for the past thirty years—good enough for us). The average H&M store's revenues are 30 percent higher than The Gap and more than double The Limited.

In 1990, $10,000 invested in H&M shares was worth more than $5 million ten years later. At the end of 1999, the Boston Consulting Group named H&M one of the top ten wealth creators in the world, behind Dell Computer but ahead of Microsoft, Schwab, and Nokia.

But the most impressive number at H&M is inventory turn. While most fashion retailers cross their fingers and hope to turn their stock four times annually— and The Gap's five turns a year is considered stellar—H&M turns their goods eight times a year (as reported by *Forbes Global Business and Finance*, May 3, 1999). That's like running a three-minute mile. How can they be so fast?

ELIMINATE THE SPEED BUMPS

Our investigation revealed that H&M has three competitive advantages that allow them to get to market faster than anyone else. Some readers will be disappointed to learn that H&M doesn't have a top-secret factory manned by automatons capable of designing and fabricating garments overnight. Instead, the competitive advantages that allow H&M to be first to market is their ruthless elimination of the speed bumps that slow other fashion retailers—and most other companies—down:

- They play their own game.

- They eliminate the middle people.

- Company executives know what's *really* happening.

PLAY YOUR OWN GAME

One of the biggest speed bumps companies face occurs when they go public. The rush of cash is good for the corporate coffers, but the big price paid for the cash infusion is trying to keep armies of stock market analysts and share buyers happy.

Stefan Persson, H&M's largest shareholder and chairperson, doesn't play the game. In fact, he refuses to play, and that represents one of H&M's biggest competitive advantages.

Most publicly traded companies have a cadre of people to patronize financial analysts and journalists in hopes of maintaining a good buzz for their share price. H&M has never called an analysts' meeting and analysts get the quarterly profit figures the same time as everyone else.

When you buy shares in H&M, you're investing solely in the ability of Stefan Persson to be a good merchant, achieve a high return on invested capital, and provide you a quarterly earnings report. The company refuses to waste time sucking up to the investment community. They need the time to be merchants rather than bankers.

Fabian Mansson, the firm's former CEO, became unnerved when we asked him to compare his company to The Gap: "Look, how would we know how The Gap is doing and why would we care? If you want to know what they're doing, go and get a copy of their financial report and compare it to ours. It's not something we follow. We refuse to follow the competition. We do our own thing." When we pushed him further and asked him if H&M could maintain their high margins, he responded tersely:

> We don't consider margin to be a goal. Maybe our margins are too high. Our business is about getting to market fast and selling garments as fast as we can. If we can lower our margins and sell even more, that, in the long run, would be even better for us. We refuse to fixate on margin as others do. We thrive on money—how much is in the pot at the end of the year—not maintaining an average margin. We refuse to target percentages.

By not paying attention to the financial markets or the competition, everyone at H&M is free to spend all their time concentrating on getting to market fast and turning the inventory eight times annually.

There's another game that H&M doesn't play. They know they are a fashion retailer, not a fashion trendsetter, and they are as ruthless about the elimination of individual and corporate ego as they are expenses. The designers and merchandisers of other fashion retailers spend much of their time attending runway, fashion, and trade shows, trying to come up with the next season's hot seller. In stark contrast, H&M representatives never attend fashion or trade shows.

Unlike many other fashion retailers who seem more interested in the accolades of their peers than financial performance, Mansson maintains that H&M never strives to set fashion:

> We don't attempt to set trends. We aren't big enough to simply put an item in our stores and drive the market. We're prepared to step aside and let anyone else who has had a successful season be seen as the expert and happily allow them to enjoy their moment in the spotlight. Meanwhile, we'll continue to do what we do and ask ourselves, "What will people be wearing six to twelve months from now?" and figure out how to get it produced as quickly and inexpensively with the highest quality as we possibly can.

Rather than wasting time building friendships with and trying to impress their competitors, the designers of H&M are directed to work the streets, shop other stores to study what people are buying, read lifestyle magazines, attend movies, and hang out in bars, nightclubs, and street festivals to observe the way people live.

ELIMINATE THE MIDDLE PEOPLE AND HAVE A HUGE POOL OF SUPPLIERS

Once H&M decides on a proposed design, the company's fifteen production offices go to work and begin negotiating with their 1,600 suppliers. The company has never purchased a finished product through a middle person. They want neither the same merchandise nor price points sold in other stores. Instead, H&M designs and produces merchandise under twenty of their own brand names.

In order to win H&M's business, suppliers must be prepared

for hard negotiations, deliver faster than they do for other retailers, and adhere to H&M's rigid demand for quality. If H&M learns of a comparable product produced for a competitor for less money, the supplier won't be used again. Similarly, if the supplier is unable to distribute and deliver the goods when promised, the relationship with H&M will be terminated.

In return for performing as agreed, suppliers are paid as agreed—something notoriously uncommon in the fashion business—and the promise of an even larger amount of business from H&M is constantly dangled in front of them. Because of the sheer size of the H&M supplier pool, all 1,600 manufacturers know they're required to constantly compete on price, quality, and speed to market.

We suspect, but were unable to prove, that H&M's production offices also serve as a significant source of ideas for the company. It stands to reason that a current or prospective supplier would be only too happy to accidentally provide *value added* in the form of information about what other retailers were planning on producing.

KNOW WHAT'S REALLY HAPPENING

Recognizing that little of a substantive nature can take place in a company unless driven by those at the top, one of H&M's important competitive advantages is that everyone—including all corporate executives—work the sales floor every week. A few years ago on the day after Thanksgiving, the CEO of one U.S. department store chain rented a large motor home, filled it with executives and a case of champagne, and toured all the company's stores in the San Francisco region. Having an entourage of suits drop in on the busiest day of the retail sales year reeking of liquor probably didn't help the employees' morale or the executives to get their finger on the pulse of the sales floor.

Echoing the words of General George Patton, who said, "You'll never know what's going on in war unless you can hear the whistle of the bullets," Fabian Mansson can't imagine a retail organization being fast when its leaders are out of touch: "Being on the sales floor is the life nerve of this business. Any company executive not on the floor isn't getting accurate information." Mansson explains: "A leader needs to be connected to the merchandise and be in touch with people's feelings and initial reactions to the goods they're selling. If you want to have a fast organization, it's deadly important to see firsthand how staff and customers are reacting to the merchandise."

When someone from the executive ranks of a company sees a product selling faster than anticipated and requests the supplier to shave two weeks off the production schedule, there's likely to be an entirely different response than if the call were placed by a reorder clerk in the planning department.

FAST-TO-MARKET COMPANIES OWN THEIR COMPETITIVE ADVANTAGE

Charles Schwab decided technology was his firm's competitive advantage and decided to own it. Hennes and Mauritz made the decisions to never deal with middle people, to have a huge pool of suppliers constantly in competition with one another, to try never to be a trendsetter, and to stay close to the action by having every executive work the sales floor.

One of the tactics used by companies that specialize in getting to market fast is their refusal to give up, sell, or have usurped from them the things that provide them a competitive advantage.

[**A SIXTY-SECOND HEADS-UP**] ➡

- When companies outsource, they run the risk of losing their competitive advantage(s).

- Owning your competitive advantage(s) helps eliminate speed bumps.

- List your business's competitive advantages:

    1._____

    2._____

    3._____

GET VENDORS AND SUPPLIERS
TO MOVE FAST

When you want to get to market fast and you're relying on vendors, suppliers, and subcontractors for vital components or parts, your chance of achieving your deadline is compromised because you're relying on others. You aren't in charge of your own destiny. Selecting the most appropriate tactic for getting everyone on your timetable depends on the size, scope, and future prospects of your business. In studying the fastest to market companies in the world we uncovered three radically different tactical approaches used. The one you select and implement will have far-reaching consequences for your business.

PLAY ON THEIR GREED—MAINTAIN A BIG POOL OF SUPPLIERS

As explored in the previous chapter, one tactic for the achievement of being fast to market—as perfected by H&M—is to maintain a mammoth base of suppliers and contractors and make them compete for every deal based on their ability to deliver on your timetable. In order to maintain a big pool of suppliers and have them all prepared to come knocking on your door whenever you call, you'd better be big enough to be a serious player. A large bakery might maintain a pool of fifteen vendors for flour. For a single bagel shop to maintain that many vendors would be humorous. Suppliers would laugh at the owner.

To make this tactic work effectively, the customer has to have a large flow of work to use like a carrot on a stick with the vendor playing the role of the donkey. The stated or implied message is the same: "Pull out the stops and deliver on my timetable and I promise—*not in writing of course*—a larger share of our work in the future." Provided the customer pays as agreed—or occasionally earlier than agreed in order to really make the supplier salivate—this tactic is best employed by large companies whose business volume will be an added persuasion.

Depending on the size of the enterprise, the employment of this tactic requires a number of employees whose sole job responsibility is to pit one vendor against another, measure performance, and negotiate constantly.

SWITCH SUPPLIERS FREQUENTLY—LET THEM GIVE AWAY THE STORE

In Part II, we explained that one tactic used by fast companies to ensure their managers remain mentally agile and decisive is to frequently switch portfolios. By changing areas of responsibility, often both the manager in charge and the people within the business unit remain constantly on their toes. The same tactic can be used with vendors and suppliers.

Most executives (based on our experience we'd estimate far more than 90 percent) only remember one line of Peter Drucker: "The purpose of business is to *find* a customer"; never read Harvard's Theodore Levitt, who wrote: "The purpose of business is to create *and keep* a customer"; and have largely ignored our advice that, "The purpose of business is to find, keep, *and grow the right customer.*"

The result is that most companies place undue emphasis on finding new business. They increase sales commissions for new business and most will give away the store to get a new customer in the misguided belief that the new customer will be unwilling to switch vendors. Companies that want to get to market faster than their competition can use this naiveté to their advantage.

By making the required delivery dates as important as quality and price in the negotiation, and by building into the agreement severe financial penalties in the event the dates are missed, new vendors and suppliers will bend over backward to comply. This tactic isn't foolproof. Sometimes, because of their exuberance over the possibility of landing a new client, vendors will promise everything and deliver nothing in spite of contracted financial penalties for nonperformance.

Caveat emptor! Make certain the prospective supplier has the capability for delivering as promised and make the penalties for nonperformance severe. Then, when it's time to reorder, even if the delivery, quality, and price were delivered as promised, use another supplier and use all the concessions granted by the first vendor as the starting point in your negotiation.

When quizzed by the supplier as to why you're using someone else, simply state that the other vendor was able to do an even better job of getting you the goods or completing the project on time and that you'll consider them again in the future.

EXCLUSIVE RELATIONSHIPS

Exclusive arrangements with vendors and suppliers offer the promise of great personal relationships, but there are risks as well. When a company has a vendor or supplier that understands and buys into what they're attempting to accomplish, consistently pulling out the stops to deliver as agreed, exclusive relationships can work well for both parties.

Unfortunately, most exclusive arrangements with suppliers and vendors occur by default. A business begins using a new supplier, is generally pleased, develops a personal relationship with the supplier, and then everyone becomes lazy and wonders why their competition is beating them to market. Your company's business is being taken for granted. And there are other risks. Consider the case of Burger King and their exclusive relationship with the supplier that stocked and delivered the fast-food giant's meat patties, condiments, even the toys used for promotional giveaways. By the middle of 1999, many Burger King restaurants in the United States found themselves running out of everything they needed to make and sell hamburgers. It seems the supplier, Ameriserve, was in big financial trouble—months later, they declared bankruptcy—and Burger King spent the rest of the year scrambling to find alternative suppliers.

If speed to market is the objective, the only way that long-term exclusive relationships with vendors and suppliers will work is if both companies share complimentary causes and guiding principles. The companies must also have detailed knowledge of each other's financial status. If speed to market is the sole objective, switching vendors and suppliers frequently and playing on most businesses' voracious appetite for new business is the most useful tactic to employ.

[**A SIXTY-SECOND HEADS-UP**] ➡

- When fast-to-market companies use outside vendors and suppliers for key components or services, they must get them on the same timetable.
- There are three tactics for getting vendors and suppliers on your timetable:
    1. Maintain a large pool of suppliers and play them against one another for speed to market.
    2. Count on most companies' willingness to make concessions for new business and frequently switch suppliers.
    3. Build exclusive relationships with like-minded people and companies.

STAY BENEATH THE RADAR

While many of the tactics employed by fast-to-market companies vary, they all share one strategy. Whether it's AOL's Steve Case doing a hundred-billion-plus-dollar deal to acquire Time Warner in only a couple of months... Sabeer Bhatia hatching an idea for Hotmail and bringing it to market within months... Leo Pujals driving Telepizza from a single location to more than 1,000 in less than ten years... Or Charles Schwab taking a demonstration from a research group into a marketable product that would forever change the company within six months... All fast-to-market companies demonstrate the ability to keep their collective mouths shut, create and perfect new products and services in secrecy, and stay beneath the radar.

Being able to act in secrecy is quickly becoming the single most important competitive advantage for companies who want to get to market first and/or fast.

LOOSE LIPS MAKE SPEED BUMPS

When companies fail to stay beneath the radar, they inadvertently create unnecessary and potentially disastrous distractions, all of which waste time and slow the enterprise down:

- When competitors learn of your plans, they might recruit key knowledge workers and team leaders who have valuable proprietary information.

- The competition might steal the complete idea and beat you to market.

- When people inside a company learn of the plans and that they have been excluded for various reasons, they may campaign against the idea or lobby to have the sharp edges taken off.

- When a company's plans become known in advance, generally the marketplace sets their expectations too high and becomes disappointed. This often results in unhappy customers and bad press.

- If another firm learns about unique processes and copies them or steals the entire idea, companies run the risk of losing all their lead time.

- Funding for the project or the ability to raise future capital may be jeopardized if other competitors appear.

- The sooner word leaks and another company can duplicate your efforts, you risk losing the benefits traditionally enjoyed by being first to market.

OPERATING IN STEALTH IS GETTING HARDER TO DO

Consider the conditions that exist today that didn't exist a decade ago:

THE INSATIABLE APPETITE FOR GOOD PRESS AND BUZZ

Conventional wisdom dictates that the more frequently a company receives favorable press, the more legitimate and successful it must be in the eyes of the market. Most companies love being written about and are on a constant prowl for good press. In addition, most executives and managers of publicly traded companies are reliant on steadily improving share prices for the bulk of their compensation.

The net effect is that in most companies it's easy to find a blabbermouth who in the name of good press or a higher share price will gladly spill the beans.

THOUSANDS OF EXTRA BUSINESS JOURNALISTS AND ANALYSTS

There are hundreds—perhaps thousands—of business cable channels, paper publications, and business Web sites that didn't exist a few years ago. Each employs scores of journalists to scoop the competition with the inside story. Businesses and all the activities in which they're engaged are under closer scrutiny than at any time in history.

AN "EAT OR BE EATEN" BUSINESS CLIMATE

Every company wants to get to market fast, beat the competition to the punch, and scare off potential rivals. Few companies are above being actively involved in intelligence gathering, "borrowing" an idea from another company, claiming it as "their own" and running with it as fast as they can.

INSTANTANEOUS COMMUNICATION

While e-mail and file attachments have dramatically altered the way people communicate, the Internet and most Intranets aren't secure, and prying eyes are generally able to find copies of whatever documents they want. A copy of an e-purchase order signaling your marketing plans will likely be on your competitor's desktop computer within hours of being received by your supplier.

OVEREAGER DEAL MAKERS DON'T KEEP SECRETS

Recently two giants in agricultural supply announced an agricultural marketplace called Rooster.com. But when several of the existing agricultural Web sites heard the news, they learned something else: their dealmakers had leaked critical intelligence.

For months, two of the companies behind Rooster.com had been picking the brains of the venture capitalists and deal makers from Farmbid.com, DirectAg.com, and XSAg.com, among others. Everybody was so hot for deep-pocket partnerships that they disclosed their research and strategy. Their future competitors simply took this free reconnaissance and handily created their own site in direct competition.

STAY BENEATH THE RADAR OR RISK BEING SHOT DOWN

Here's how a few fast companies used secrecy as a competitive advantage.

HOTMAIL

When Sabeer Bhatia came up with the concept for Hotmail, he and partner Jack Smith knew that all they possessed was a simple idea: anyone with access to the Internet would be able to keyboard in the Hotmail address, enter their password, and, for *free*, receive e-mail from any other computer on the planet with Internet access. The duo realized that before long the same idea would occur to someone else. Even more frightening was the prospect that this person might be a staffer of Microsoft, Netscape, or IBM, or someone bringing the idea to a company with technology and deep pockets.

Bhatia offers a textbook lesson in staying beneath the radar. First, Bhatia and Smith needed to raise some money to fund the project. But they knew that if the wrong person learned of their idea, they'd be dead before they started. Bhatia pitched and asked hundreds of people for money without revealing the real idea: "I turned over every stone looking for money. Anyone who would listen, I'd talk to. I pitched friends, colleagues, classmates, partners, anyone, anywhere, anytime. I pitched a Texas millionaire, an oil magnate, a real estate person, and even a venture capitalist who funded gas stations."

But Bhatia would only reveal the *big* idea after he was certain he wasn't being rejected for some trivial or irrelevant reason: "All potential investors got the same pitch—for Java Soft, another program we'd played with. If the person I started to sell started spouting reasons that I believed were silly ones for rejecting us, they never got to hear about the real idea. Eventually only four people knew about our real plan."

When he'd finally raised $300,000, he needed to begin recruiting staff. He knew the money he'd raised wasn't enough, so he had to attract people in return for giving them small pieces of the company. Because these employees had a vested financial interest in the success of the company and knew they'd end up with nothing if the idea were stolen, maintaining their secrecy wasn't a problem. Hourly and clerical workers were never told the real nature of the company's business.

During the eight months it took the firm to find an office, hire staff, write the code, and prepare the product, Bhatia and Smith remained convinced that either the idea would occur to someone else—maybe it already had—or that someone would steal their idea. They kept one trump card to play if either scenario occurred:

> We originally thought we'd charge a small monthly fee like $4.95 for the service, but we quickly determined that another company could match it or beat the price and we'd be dead, so we decided the service would be free. We'd make our money selling advertising and by selling the demographic details of the services users, much like a direct mail house sells lists of consumers.

By the time Hotmail signed on, July 4 1996, fewer than thirty people knew what the company was about. Eighteen months later, Hotmail had more than 20 million customers, and, still paranoid and secretive, Bhatia knew he had to make a move: either sell the company or transform it into a major portal site. Within days, a deal was cut with Microsoft, and Bhatia and Smith walked away with $440 million. There is no question in Bhatia's mind that had word leaked, Hotmail would not have been first to market nor would it have been a huge success.

CHARLES SCHWAB

In late 1995, Dawn Lepore, Charles Schwab's CTO, invited Chuck Schwab to a demonstration being conducted by one of the company's research groups. The group wanted to demonstrate a piece of software they'd created that would allow one Schwab computer to talk to another.

As soon as Schwab and Lepore saw the demonstration, they realized the implication: a Schwab customer could place an order on her PC and have the trade executed and confirmation returned without any manual entries being required. A project team was immediately authorized to get Web trading up and running. The group was assigned a code name, a leader was assigned, and the group began their work in total secrecy. Bypassing the company's hierarchy, the head of the group reported directly to Dave Pottruck. Within six months, the company was ready to debut e.schwab. While E*trade and a host of other companies were still playing with the technology, stodgy Schwab beat them to the punch because of their ability to keep a secret.

H&M

The magic of H&M is their mastery of the 1,600 vendors and suppliers managed out of the firm's fifteen worldwide production offices.

H&M dismisses the notion that they're secretive, pointing out that everything they do is on display daily in every one of their stores. What they fail to add is that it would be easier for a skunk to snag an invitation to a dinner party at the White House than it would be to get deep inside H&M's production offices and watch them work.

The production offices are the company's nerve centers. They're where distribution logistics are determined, patterns for clothing are stored, and intelligence from their vendors is received. Recognizing the slim competitive advantage they enjoy, the production offices are off limits to everyone but H&M staffers with security clearance.

HOW TO KEEP A SECRET

When Arthur Wellesley was a young general in India, the emissary of an Indian ruler was anxious to learn what territories might be ceded to his master as a result of a treaty. Having tried various approaches and finding that the general could not be drawn to the subject, the emissary finally offered Wellesley a huge bribe for the information. Leaning toward the emissary, Wellesley whispered in his ear, "Can you keep a secret?" "Yes, indeed," said the Indian eagerly. "So can I," deadpanned the future duke of Wellington.

Times have changed in the 200 years since the duke kept a secret merely because he felt honor bound to do so. Special tactics are used by companies that are able to keep secrets and stay beneath the radar.

TURN FAST TO MARKET
INTO A CRUSADE

In the cases of AOL, H&M, Charles Schwab, and Hotmail, everyone on the team was made to feel they were important contributors to something of significance. While neither gobbling up Time Warner, turning your goods eight times a year, nor e-trading will change the world, all team members bought into a cause and joined a crusade that they knew would be successful only if it remained a secret.

LET EVERYONE UNDERSTAND THAT "DUMB
IS SMART AND SMART IS DUMB"

One line in Puzo and Coppola's screenplay for *The Godfather* made a lasting impression on us. Sollozzo, a powerful drug supplier, had just met with the Corleone family to entice the Don into a partnership. The Don turned him down. As the meeting broke up, the Don pulled Sonny aside. Sonny had made a comment in the meeting to show Sollozzo that he and his family were not fools and he was tough enough to say so. Sharply rebuking him for being up front and revealing with someone who could become the future enemy, the Don concluded, "Never tell anybody outside the family what you're thinking again!" Don Corleone was telling his son that dumb is smart and smart is dumb.

We can't avoid friends, suppliers, the media, potential rivals, and future customers. But we can suppress the urge to "telegraph" our thoughts and competencies by simply acting impressed with what we're told and responding nonchalantly.

Make certain team members understand they can hurt everything you have worked for if knowledge of the project, company, or undertaking becomes public. Help them see that every conversation must be analyzed and no one "outside the family" deserves information. Teach everyone the value of being underestimated!

FINANCIALLY REWARD PEOPLE FOR
SUCCESSFULLY KEEPING THE SECRET

When people have a vested financial interest in the successful completion of a project, they're more likely to be willing to stay beneath the radar.

MAKE LEAKING THE SECRET A PUNISHABLE OFFENSE

Make maintaining secrecy a job requirement and promptly fire anyone who violates the agreement.

CONSTANTLY REMIND PEOPLE OF THE SIGNIFICANCE
OF WHAT THEY'RE ACCOMPLISHING

In the fast-to-market companies we studied, team leaders and members were constantly reminded of the significance of the work in which they were involved and the risks if the real nature of the work became public knowledge.

[A SIXTY-SECOND HEADS-UP]

- The greater the number of people who learn about your planned product or service, the greater the number of distractions you'll encounter.

- Operating in stealth is becoming increasingly complex and demands specially designed tactics to ensure your secret is kept.

- When pitching for money or venture capital, never reveal the real idea until you're certain you're not being rejected for the sake of being rejected.

- Tell as few people as possible about your plans and processes.

KEEP IT SIMPLE

*H*erb (a true story; name has been changed) was a swimming pool installation foreman, who in the late 1980s decided to go into business for himself. He slapped a second mortgage on the family home and picked up $100,000 with which to begin his business.

In spite of a bad economy, his first few years were good ones. Installing an average of fifty in-ground pools annually, Herb was respected and had figured out how to build great pools while making a tidy profit. Before long, Herb was earning almost $100,000 a year.

By the early 1990s, Herb's appetite had grown and he decided to expand his business. His neighbors had bigger homes, took fancier vacations, and their kids went to better schools. Herb figured he could increase his revenues by creating a new division of the company that would do the landscaping around the pools he sold. Shortly after his foray into landscaping, about which he knew nothing and in which he had little interest other than money, he also decided to start a pool maintenance company that would service the pools he built. "Why leave money on the table?" he frequently laughed rhetorically.

As suitable for a man in his position—a business owner with three divisions—Herb quickly acquired a BMW, the house was remodeled, and the kids were placed in more expensive schools. Before long, Herb's lack of knowledge about both landscaping and pool maintenance became obvious and he took in two partners to manage these parts of the business. When neither took off as planned, Herb propped them up with earnings from pool installation.

Over the next six years, everything that could go wrong did. Inept partners had fleeced him, he'd opened and closed a pool chemical retail location, he had scores of business managers, all of whom intimidated him, bills went unpaid, monies intended for payroll taxes were used to shore up the business, liens were placed by the government, and his key people left and started competitive pool businesses. Soon, Herb had scores of disgruntled customers. Everything was in shambles. Finally, in 1997, he closed up shop and declared bankruptcy. The last time we saw Herb, he was driving a battered pickup truck and working as a pool installer for another company.

What does the story about Herb have to do with fast to market? Plenty. Herb's business began at about the same time as Steve Case's AOL and Leo Pujal's Telepizza, and at the same time that Charles Schwab, Lowry Mays, and Stuart Hornery were gearing their companies up for explosive fast-to-market growth. Could Herb have become as successful in the swimming pool business as these men did in their respective fields? We think so . . . if only he had kept the proposition simple.

IF YOU WANT SPEED TO MARKET, KISS!

Keep it simple stupid! "Our business is a simple one and the only difference between us and our competitors is execution." Randall and Mark Mays of Clear Channel Communications made that statement. So did Steve Case of AOL. Fabian Mansson, former CEO of H&M, said the same thing. So did Sabeer Bhatia of Hotmail, Leo Pujals of Telepizza, and Stuart Hornery of Lend Lease.

As we traveled the world in search of the fastest-to-market companies and spent time with their leaders, we heard, "Our business is a simple one," over and over again. At first we thought we were witnessing humility. Later we wondered if these accomplished leaders weren't patronizing us and shining us on. Finally, we concluded they were right. Companies that are fastest to market keep their business propositions simple.

In fact, as we conducted further research, we discovered the biggest battle the leaders of fast-to-market companies have to fight is with their own people—those who would complicate the proposition given half a chance.

SPEED AND BEING FAST TO MARKET IS THE NATURAL CONDITION

Infants love the rush of quick movement. To be swung about, tossed high in the air, or sped down a path in the stroller brings big smiles and giggles. Toddlers rush everywhere, constantly charging and ignoring obstacles.

The teenage years are dominated by a frantic pursuit of fast food, fast cars, and fast friends. Even into their twenties, many people are captivated by whirlwind affairs, reckless adventures, and fast-moving sports. Fast money and quick hits in business are images that appeal to us.

Finally, the years of warning register a note and we slow down. We learn that speed flies in the face of what we're taught is wise in business. Because we're human and engage in self-fulfilling prophecy, we start building speed bumps to slow us down.

If you want to join the ranks of the fastest-to-market businesses, you must first accept that speed and being fast to market is the natural condition; it's everything most people do to put hurdles in their way that slows them down.

The biggest obstacle that slows down companies occurs when they complicate the business proposition. All the CEOs and executives who humbly proclaimed their business model as being very simple had in fact accomplished the near impossible:

- H&M moves so fast that they take a fashion designer's drawing and have the finished garment in hundreds of stores within two months.

- Lend Lease tackles impossible-to-build projects and gets them done in half the time taken by their competitors to build cookie-cutter office buildings.

- On average, Clear Channel Communications purchased four radio stations and 2,000 billboards every week for more than eight years without a week off.

- Steve Case of AOL acquired eighty companies, entered into hundreds of partnerships, and brought to market thousands of new features and destroyed his competition in the process.

- Leo Pujals started the 1990s with one pizza restaurant and no money. For the next ten years, he opened 100 restaurants each year and ended the decade with a company worth billions.

SPEED REQUIRES CONSTANT FOCUS

No communications company in the world has grown as quickly or recorded as many firsts as Clear Channel. While many other media companies had similar aspirations and tried to move as fast as Clear Channel, the blinding speed with which they acquired nearly 1,000 radio stations left the competition looking like a bunch of stunned mullets.

While their competitors were busy building elaborate infrastructures, the Mays family kept it simple. Randall Mays, who serves as the company's treasurer and CFO, says that this has been the key to Clear Channel's success:

This is a simple business and it's vital to keep it that way. In radio and television you only need to do three things. First, put a decent product on the air, which isn't that difficult to accomplish. Then, hire and motivate a sales staff. Finally, keep expenses down. That's it. We constantly remind ourselves of the simplicity of the businesses we're in and keep it that way. What ruins execution is when people try to make things more difficult than they are.

Using a sports analogy he adds:

All the major owners started the race in the same place we were—14 radio stations, the maximum you could own until deregulation. In fact, we had fewer financial resources than most of the other groups. What's allowed us to win is that we pay attention to the blocking and tackling . . . the basics. We keep it very simple and execute.

When a company achieves a modicum of success in one business, its executives often think of themselves as omnipotent and capable of running any business. The business books reveal that most often that ego-centered sense of omniscience—Herb starting a landscaping business and Quaker Oats buying Snapple—proves unfounded and the business units acquired at premium prices are later unloaded for pennies on the dollar. Even greater than the financial pain are the distractions that keep them from being fast or first to market in their core competencies.

FIGURE OUT WHAT YOU DO AND THEN DO IT OVER AND OVER, BECOMING FASTER EACH TIME

Stefan Persson and Fabian Mansson said that H&M was about fashion, quality, and price . . . and doing it fast. Everyone at H&M moves fast—sometimes simply for the sake of moving fast. Fabian Mansson says that it's H&M's fast pace that attracts other fast people:

We are a company without limits and we move at the speed of light. We don't want to hear about limits from anyone. The phones ring off the hook, people rush in and out, you need this, you need that—we move fast all the time. It's our commitment to everything being fast that makes this a great place to be. If we were to say that next year we won't open any stores, then we would be out of breath and dead.

The company has never purchased a factory, never worked with a middle person, steadfastly refuses to own the real estate where their stores are located, and has never aspired to be viewed as a fashion trendsetter. All those things would distract them from what they do: "Make educated guesses as to what people want to wear—if that includes knocking off someone else's garments, that's fine—figure out how to get quality garments produced as fast and inexpensively as is physically possible, and then sell faster and cheaper than anyone else."

H&M's magic in getting to market fast is that they've never deviated from their formula:

Anyone can walk into our stores and see exactly what we do and how we do it. We run a very simple business. Everyone wants to believe it's complicated and that we must possess big dark secrets of how we do things. We don't. We keep the model very simple and work it over and over again, always getting a little better at what we do.

HOW MUCH TIME DO YOU SPEND ON SPEED TO MARKET?

Almost a half-century ago, a satiric study of the British Army by C. Parkinson concluded that "work expands to fill the time available for its completion." We don't doubt that everyone works at slow-moving companies . . . just that they work at the work thing . . . being busy for the sake of appearing busy.

It's the speed bumps we create—complicating the original business proposition—that prevents most companies from being fast or first to market. When time is wasted in meaningless meetings and activities, and executives are seen as slow and bureaucratic, this is the example the rest of the organization will follow.

[A SIXTY-SECOND HEADS-UP]

- If you want to be fast to market, keep it simple.
- Being fast to market is the natural condition. It's the speed bumps that slow enterprises down.
- Speed requires constant focus with constant attention to the basics.
- Find and perfect a simple formula and do it over and over, becoming faster each time.
- Spend your time becoming faster, not just being busy for the sake of it.

INSTITUTIONALIZE INNOVATION

*I*n order to be fast/first to market, five things have to happen. The more simultaneously they occur, the faster to market the company will be:

- ANTICIPATE A NEW SERVICE OR PRODUCT AND MAKE A DECISION.

- QUICKLY ALLOCATE RESOURCES.

- RALLY EVERYONE BEHIND THE EFFORT.

- ELIMINATE ALL POTENTIAL SPEED BUMPS.

- GET EVERYONE ON THE REQUIRED TIMETABLE.

The problem for most businesses, big and small, is their inability to consistently get to market fast. When we began our search for the fastest-to-market companies, we reviewed published stories and case studies of thousands of businesses. We found many companies that had managed to do one or two things fast, but upon further investigation most turned out to be real Jekyll-and-Hyde stories. Kmart, P&G, Kodak, and Toys "Я" Us manage to be fast on occasion, but to hold them up as examples of speed wouldn't be credible.

If the critics dig deep enough, they may succeed in finding missteps on the part of our final selections for fastest/first-to-market companies, but one of the reasons for the inclusion of Hotmail, Clear Channel, Charles Schwab, H&M, Lend Lease, AOL, and Telepizza is that each of them has demonstrated the ability to be *consistently* fast in their respective fields. How do they do it?

SPEED REQUIRES A NONSTOP FLOW OF IDEAS

Any company where only the suits are viewed as being smart enough to come up with the ideas for innovative products, services and processes will be far slower to market than companies where everyone in the organization is involved in creating a nonstop flood of new ideas, suggestions, proposed problem solving, and innovation. Big-name companies that have recently faltered and blown out their CEOs when they were unable to speed things up include P&G, Compaq, Coca-Cola, and Bank One. It's interesting that one trait shared by all of these firms gone S-L-O-W is that they all counted *exclusively* on top management for their ideas.

John Reid, who left Coca-Cola to become CEO of Comet Systems, an Internet software company, says, "At Coca-Cola all of the ideas came from top management and then we'd form teams to try and make them work. Here [at Comet Systems] it's the people sitting outside my door who are constantly coming up with ideas."

Any business that relies on top management for all its ideas either sets up a "them against us" mentality, where the worker bees patiently wait with quiet smiles on their faces for initiatives to fail, or, over time, a complacent environment is created where everyone is willing to wait for someone above them to come up with the answer to every question. Being fast to market requires a constant flow of innovative ideas.

THE BEST IDEA WINS

Randall Mays of Clear Channel Communications credits his father Lowry's complete lack of ego for setting the tone that enables them to be fast to market with programming concepts, sales initiatives, and huge deals:

> Look, around here we have a rule. The best idea wins. Period. We don't care who it comes from.
>
> Every time we make an acquisition, the first thing we do is study what they are doing better than what we're doing and then get the word out through our monthly conference calls and meetings. We've never made an acquisition where we haven't found somebody doing things better than the way we were doing them.

In fast-to-market companies there is a lack of corporate ego and an environment that sends the message that the best idea wins.

INSTITUTIONALIZE INNOVATION

When a business *institutionalizes* a process, the method or process has become the established practice rather than the exception. Can you imagine the damage to McDonald's if every employee were allowed to handle customer transactions however they wished? Institutionalizing a process can be as simple as everyone at McDonald's being taught and expected to ask, "Would you like fries with that?"

When a process becomes institutionalized, a business is proclaiming that a method has been determined to be its *best practice*. The wheel doesn't have to be reinvented every time. Fast-to-market companies institutionalize as many processes and procedures as they can.

Is it possible to institutionalize innovation, and what does it have to do with being fast to market? We think Charles Schwab has created the best replicable model.

SCHWAB THINK

In Part I, Evelyn Dilsaver, senior VP and chief of staff at Charles Schwab, reminds us of a sad business truth: "Big ideas and innovation come from the top because that's where the resources are and that's where the power to say *yes* exists." Dilsaver contends, "Most often it's only the chair or the CEO who can push an idea with sharp edges through the company. Otherwise, everyone you pass your idea to negotiates away the sharp edges and it gets honed down to something that doesn't mean anything."

Dilsaver says that when staffers witness the constant honing away of the sharp edges from their ideas and proposed innovations, everyone begins saying, "I don't have time to innovate," or, "There's no process for having my idea heard." The tool that Dilsaver created to institutionalize innovation at Schwab is the **THINK©** (**TH**e Innovation **N**etwor**K**) Web site on Schwab's Intranet, which is available to every staff member, associate, and executive.

THINK has four different zones. In **Idea Central**, ideas are accepted from everyone. **The Loop** is used to gather proposed ideas for Schwab's Web site. **Smart** is for Schwab's telephone customer care centers. **Venture Quest** is for big revolutionary ideas.

Dilsaver has people working for her who help contributors shape their ideas into actual business plans. The person ceding the idea can give ownership of the idea away, be on the team, or, if qualified, head the team that will present the idea. According to Dilsaver, everyone submitting proposals is asked to answer ten questions on the Web site:

- Does it fit Schwab's guiding principles?

- Which strategic priority does your idea support the most (the software provides them the strategic priorities)?

- Who will benefit the most?

- What specific need or opportunity does the idea tackle?

- What's the problem being tackled?

- What are the success factors?

- What set of rules would your innovation break Schwab has found that their most successful ideas have resulted from breaking their own rules)?

- Who would your idea upset the most?

- How destructive would it be?

- Who supports the idea?

Once a quarter, Schwab's Innovation Council meets and reviews the business plans the same way a venture capitalist would, and decides which ones to fund and how much money and resources should be provided. Even the owners of ideas and innovations that don't receive approval for the pilot stage get recognition in the form of bonuses, Schwab shares, or options.

Schwab's THINK Web site democratizes innovation and invites everyone who works for the company to be an active participant in dreaming about, creating, and developing the new products and services that allow Schwab to be consistently faster to market than their competition. Schwab's THINK can be replicated by any business prepared to acknowledge the importance of a nonstop flow of ideas and to allocate sufficient resources.

[A SIXTY-SECOND HEADS-UP]➡

- Being consistently fast to market requires a nonstop flow of good ideas about products, services, and processes.
- The companies who are consistently fast to market create corporate environments where the best idea wins.
- The best-case scenario occurs when a business is able to institutionalize innovation.
- Charles Schwab's THINK Web site encourages innovation.

GET OTHER FAST PEOPLE ON YOUR SIDE

When Richard Davis, the former CEO of software developer I-market, took over the reins as head of Rand McNally, he found a slow, plodding company burdened by 150 years of speed bumps and uncertain of its future in the e-economy. Davis committed to revitalizing Rand McNally's fortunes quickly, including getting lots of products to market fast and making e-commerce a vital part of the company's future. Within weeks of his arrival, the speed bumps started to slow him down: "It takes HR a month to hire someone," he complained. "I want it done in a week."

For a company used to launching only ten new products annually, Davis set a hairy goal: the introduction of more than 120 new products during his first year in office. To meet his goal—the company ended up introducing 127 new products during his first year—Davis explains, "The only way I could speed things up was by bringing in executives and software developers from other fast companies."

David Ogilvy said, "If we hire people smaller than ourselves, we'll become a company of midgets, but if we hire people bigger than we are, we'll become a company of giants." We can deduce that hiring faster people will improve the speed of any company. No business is going to get to market fast with slow people.

AN ADMISSION OF OUR OWN CHECKERED PAST

During the past two decades, we've hired hundreds of people to work for us and have supervised the hiring of many thousands more for client companies. Along the way, we've hired some doozies, made every mistake that can be made, and have hopefully learned some valuable lessons. One of the most important lessons is that if you hire employees and it turns out they aren't moving as fast as you need them to move, there are only two possibilities:

> *THERE ARE TOO MANY SPEED BUMPS,.*
> *OR . . .*
> *YOU HIRED A TURTLE!*

The executive or manager committed to being fast to market must administer two litmus tests: the first to the organization and the second to every person working for or alongside him or her. If the people around the manager/owner/leader aren't getting to market fast enough because there are too many speed bumps, the barriers must be identified and eliminated. If the speed bumps have been removed and the organization still isn't fast enough to market, then the turtles must be dealt with.

Unfortunately, when most managers realize they've hired a turtle, they have a tendency to defend their personnel selection because their ego can't handle admitting mistakes. Remember the ancient Chinese proverb: "When you find a turtle on a pole, someone put it there."

Mark Mays, Clear Channel's president and COO, says, "In less than three weeks, start to finish, we did a $23 billion deal. That's fast to market . . . that's speed. I tell our people that anything is possible within three weeks. I won't accept an excuse of 'no' or, 'there's not enough time.' You can get anything done!"

According to Mays, when Clear Channel buys a new media property, they evaluate the management, and, within three months, if the managers in place are unable to adapt to the speed with which the rest of the company moves, they're out. "Bam, bam, bam," explains Mark Mays, "if they don't make it, if they can't move fast enough, we'll clean it up and move on to a better management team. Get rid of people who aren't going to change and move fast. As a company, we have to make those decisions quickly."

Dave Pottruck of Schwab echoes Mays's words when he talks about Schwab's approach to people and being fast: "Our entire culture is built around change and being fast. If you don't like speed and change, then don't work here."

Leo Pujals, the founder of Telepizza, says, "You can't be fast to market with a new product, a new advertising campaign, or a new restaurant unless you are surrounded with people who move with a sense of urgency in everything they do."

HOPING TO BE HIT WITH A MAGIC STICK—
THE SEARCH FOR FAST PEOPLE

Anyone who has ever performed a consulting job, taught a class, or counseled a friend or relative knows that many people go through life and business looking for someone else to provide them a set of easy answers. We're constantly asked how companies can go about finding and keeping fast people. Even worse are those who call and want to know if we're aware of any fast-to-market people they can poach from other companies. The question reveals not only their laziness but their naiveté as well.

There are lots of fast people. As we already pointed out, speed is the natural condition. The real question a company should ask is what can it do to attract speedy, fast-to-market people.

BIRDS OF THE FEATHER HANG TOGETHER

For the past decade, hundreds of thousands of young college and business school graduates have been forgoing the chance to join reliable, steady, secure companies with household names in favor of high-risk start-ups. At the same time, up-and-coming leaders at old-line companies have been jumping ship in droves to join new ventures. Is it simply the lure of a high-stakes game where winners can walk with millions? We don't think so.

As studied and reported for years by anthropologists, people like to be around others who share their values, their view of the world, and ambitions. If you want to attract fast people capable of bringing services and products to market faster than the competition, then the business unit must be viewed as fast. Toss hard-charging, fast-to-market leaders from H&M into a stodgy old department store, tell them to get the place fast to market, and they wouldn't know what to do. Chances are that upon witnessing the countless bureaucratic roadblocks they'd bolt. Put team leaders from Lend Lease in charge of a building project for a staid old-world construction company and tell them to build it in half the time (as Lend Lease routinely does) and without their fast-to-market infrastructure supporting them, they might not know where to begin.

One of the peculiarities we uncovered at fast-to-market companies is that although their personnel turnover rate is higher in the first few months of employment than their slower-paced counterparts, once someone has made the cut and is comfortable in a take-no-prisoners environment, he or she seldom leaves. Mark Mays of Clear Channel sums up the refrain we heard from all fast-to-market companies: "I can count on two hands the number of our managers who we wanted to keep but left us, and most of those retired on their multimillion-dollar Clear Channel portfolios." Ditto for Hotmail, Lend Lease, AOL, Schwab, Telepizza, and H&M.

HOW TO FIND, KEEP, AND GROW FAST-TO-MARKET PEOPLE

Here are tactics used by the fastest-to-market companies:

- Invite people to join a crusade, not take a job.

- Get rid of the internal speed bumps. Fast people are notoriously intolerant of bureaucracy.

- Have strong centralized financial controls. Fast people have been known to disregard budgetary constraints in favor of speed.

- Keep close score. Fast people are competitors. Leo Pujals of Telepizza likens a company without a daily score-board—where everyone can see the score—to competing in or watching a basketball game where no score is kept.

- Provide big financial incentives. Generously share the wealth in return for the achievement of the agreed objectives. The days of people laboring for months for a $1,000 bonus don't exist anymore.

- Regularly acknowledge and celebrate the achievements of fast-to-market staffers and leaders. Despite protestations to the contrary, everyone loves hearing the sound of their name followed by the description of their accomplishment.

- Keep moving the bar or they'll leave. Fast people won't be content with doing the same thing day after day, year after year. Switch their portfolios frequently.

[**A SIXTY-SECOND HEADS-UP**]

- When people aren't moving fast, it's either because there are speed bumps blocking their path or you've hired a turtle.

- If you find a turtle on a pole, someone put it there.

- Fast people want to associate with other fast people.

- There are seven tactics used by fast companies for finding, keeping, and growing fast people.

PART IV

SUSTAINING SPEED

Almost all companies are able to point with pride to one or two episodes in the past when they successfully mustered the resources and everyone or almost everyone got the job done. It felt great—that's why people continue to talk about big victories years after the fact. There are too few of them.

But a few businesses are constantly fast and first to market, viewed by everyone as innovative, scoring one big win after another, and achieving huge growth year after year. The executives and leaders of these companies become wealthy, they get all the good press, and their investors/shareholders love them. It appears they've been the recipients of every lucky break.

Are they simply lucky? Were they just in the right place at the right time? Can it be as effortless as they make it appear? Nope! In the course of our research we discovered nine tactics used by the fastest companies to sustain speed. This is the magic almost any business can employ to maintain velocity:

- PROVE THE MATH.

- BE RUTHLESS WITH RESOURCES.

- USE A CENTRAL SCOREBOARD.

- STAY FINANCIALLY FLEXIBLE.

- USE NARRATIVES AND STORIES.

- PLAY YOUR OWN GAME.

- DON'T B.S. YOURSELF.

- ADAPT, IMPROVISE, AND OVERCOME.

- STAY CLOSE TO THE CUSTOMER.

PROVE THE MATH

*I*n 1999, we were huddled in a retreat with a group of powerful television executives. These men and women were the general managers of television stations in medium to major markets across the United States.

If you don't know much about being the general manager of a television station, take our word for it—there's not a better gig. The compensation package is generally several hundred thousand dollars (or more) annually. The job title carries prestige.

For many years, the general managers of television stations didn't have to fret about revenues. Between the networks paying them to carry their programming, strong national and regional advertising buys placed by advertising agencies, and the rest of the available time sold by salespeople to local businesses, a steady revenue stream was assured. Now, with the lightning-fast nature of change on the media landscape, there's not a television executive who isn't concerned with exercising a greater degree of control over his or her destiny by increasing sales to local businesses ASAP. This recognition led us to one of the questions we asked the assembled group of general managers: "How many sales calls should a salesperson make in a typical day?"

Everyone had an opinion. "Ten a day, barked an old man from the back of the room—that's what I used to make when I started in the business."

"No way," countered a "politically correct" from the West Coast. "I've never worked in sales, but intuitively I know that's too many. I'd rather have my people make fewer quality calls than many of them for which they weren't prepared."

On and on it went. Everyone had a number and was prepared to defend their choice. Finally, tongue in cheek, we asked if the group could reach a consensus. After a lot of wrangling, they did. They decided that their salespeople should be able to make and keep seven appointments a day.

Because our work wasn't a one-time effort but part of a major change initiative, and we'd be together again in less than a month, we asked the general managers how many of them would be willing to spend one full week doing nothing else but making sales calls. The hands in the air were few until the group nervously looked around and saw the raised hand of the CEO. After a few hard gulps, everyone slowly raised their hand.

The next time we got together, our first question was, "What should the MSP—minimum standard of performance—be for the number of sales calls made daily by a salesperson?" Having spent a full week making sales calls, the group knew how to answer. This time, the discussion was short and to the point. Within minutes, the group agreed that a salesperson could make four productive face-to-face calls daily.

"If we've proven that you can make four calls a day, then that's what the number needs to be," one of the managers said strongly, concluding, "It's a waste of time telling people to do something that hasn't been proven possible!" Within the next thirty days, the MSP of four sales a day was introduced at all the stations and predictably revenues soared. None of the salespeople—many of whom were actually making only one or two calls a day—were able to offer excuses as to why four calls a day weren't possible. After all, the head people had proven the math.

DON'T PENCIL YOURSELF INTO OBLIVION

Lots of entrepreneurs, executives, and managers of business pencil themselves into oblivion, silently dreaming, *Wow, if we mail out 100,000 brochures and get an 8 percent response, and if only half of those people buy what we're selling and the average selling price is $5,000, that's $20 million.* In their dreams these people are already vacationing on a tropical beach.

Although there's nothing inherently wrong with dreaming, more often than not the exuberant mental meanderings of the suits become the targets that other people are expected to achieve. Then, when the goals aren't realized, there are repercussions, reviews, reallocation of resources, shutdowns in production, suppliers left holding the bag, and a host of unhappy people.

Fast leaders, as opposed to slow managers, prove the math. It's what gives them the right to be leaders.

IF YOU WANT TO STAY FAST, PROVE THE MATH

One of the most engaging personalities we got to know during our research was Leo Pujals, the founder of Telepizza, who presided over his company's growth from one Madrid pizza restaurant to more than 1,000 in less than ten years. Cuban born, American raised, and a Spanish citizen, Pujals is an intense, passionate man given to storytelling and larger-than-life gestures. As he explains, his decision to leave a cushy job at Johnson & Johnson and risk his life savings on a pizza restaurant, was possible because he proved the math:

> So there I was. I took every penny I had and made plans to open the restaurant.
>
> For weeks, the neighborhood kids would come 'round and bang on the door wanting to know when we'd open for business. I kept shooing them away, telling them we'd open when we had perfected the best pizza in the world.
>
> One day, they came back again and I got an idea. I invited them in for pizza and told them the pizza was free if they'd come back every day until they were able to say it was the best in the world. So, every day these kids would show up and I'd make them pizza, and finally, after a couple of weeks, they all agreed the pizza I'd made them that day was the best in world. Then I knew I was ready to open for business.

Pujals's answer for the dilemma of how to deliver pizza on Madrid's notoriously narrow urban streets was to deliver it by bicycle and scooter. To get the word out, he had the delivery people begin stuffing neighborhood mailboxes with promotional fliers. Keeping an accurate count of the number of fliers delivered and the number of orders received, within months Pujals knew precisely how many fliers had to be delivered each day in order to receive the desired number of telephone orders.

Next, he went to work on increasing the average order size and personally worked the telephones in the back of the restaurant, answering calls, taking orders, and asking, "Would you like extra cheese on your pizza?" Again, he maintained accurate logs of how many calls were received and which percentage opted for the purchase of extra cheese.

Soon another question was added to the repertoire: "Would you like garlic bread with your pizza?" Again, Pujals kept track of every call received and the number of callers who purchased garlic bread.

In Spain almost all businesses find themselves in a discounting war, and Pujals was mindful of the competition. His answer was to match the discount coupons offered by other pizza restaurants. Having discovered that most of his customers had children, he began buying vast lots of small toys, flashlights, and videotapes and asking, "Would you like the Kiddie Toy Pack with your pizza?" The Kiddie Toy Pack was free with regular-priced pizzas. Again, Pujals kept meticulous records of every telephone call and every sale.

As profits began to mount, Pujals realized what he possessed—he knew how many fliers had to be delivered each day to maximize sales, he knew exactly what percentage of callers would buy add-on sales items, he knew exactly what his costs were and what his profits would be. *He had a replicable blueprint for success.*

If he opened another restaurant, he reasoned, and did things *exactly* the same way in the second location, the restaurant would become an instant success. Between the profits from the first restaurant, the proceeds from the sale of his car (for more than a year, Pujals, the former big-time executive, tooled around Madrid on a scooter), and bringing in his brother as a partner, Pujals pulled together the resources for a second restaurant. It was a smashing success!

Pujals recounts those dizzying months: "There I was driving my scooter between the restaurants, making certain that everything was done exactly the same in both locations, and if the numbers were off even a fraction it was because somebody wasn't doing what I'd proven could be done."

A small bank loan allowed Pujals to open two more locations and franchising provided the company the financial resources to continue its fast growth, but according to Pujals one thing never changed: "We knew the math . . . we had proven it. We knew exactly how many fliers it took to generate the number of calls we needed. We knew exactly what percentage of callers would buy extra cheese, toppings, garlic bread, and toys if asked. It was a foolproof set of math."

Any manager who deviated from Pujals's proven math got a private one-on-one with the man himself. One private meeting with Pujals generally worked. If a second meeting was required, the manager was fired.

The managers who were able to implement Pujals's math and keep expenses under control made more money than they'd ever hoped for and became, in Pujals's words, "Telepizza citizens out to conquer the world." Even with hundreds of restaurants, Pujals and a handful of lieutenants—all who had personally proven the math—were able to look at the previous day's reports and immediately know which restaurants hadn't delivered a sufficient number of fliers the previous day and which did not ask the proven questions.

In spite of a fiery temper and a zero tolerance for not following the company's blueprint for success, Pujals is revered and loved by everyone in the company. As we heard repeatedly, "Leo never asked anyone to do anything he hadn't done or proven could be done. We all move fast because Leo moves fast." All that separated Leo Pujals from the hundreds of thousands of would-be pizza kings is that his personally proven operating formula became the most important ingredient in his pizza.

THE INHERENT DANGER IN PROVEN MATH AND FORMULAS

In order to remain valid, the math must be regularly retested by the business leadership. Otherwise, the math simply becomes "the way we do things here and we're not allowed to change it."

In the late 1960s, car dealers in the United States began using a turnover system (TO) to sell cars. One salesperson would meet and greet the customers and land them on a car, but when it was time to negotiate the deal the customers were TOed to a "closer." If the closer couldn't complete the deal, the customers were TOed to yet another salesperson or manager, and on and on. Finally, when the deal was done, the customers would be turned over to still another salesperson for add-on sales.

The introduction of many new faces into the negotiating process substantially improved both closing rates and gross profit margins for dealers. Many dealers proved the math and discovered they were able to close one out of four "ups" (customers walking into the showroom) with the TO system.

Throughout the 1970s and 1980s, the math held and most car dealers were able to nail one out of four people walking onto their lot. In the 1990s, things changed. As many women were purchasing cars as men, and, as a group, they were offended by the hard-sell nature of the TO system.

With the advent of the Internet, potential customers were able to log on to a variety of Web sites and find out what the dealer had actually paid the factory for the car, and the manufacturers were grading their dealers as much on their ability to satisfy customers as to sell cars. By 1995, there were three times the number of makes and models than had been available just decades before and consumers had more choices. These factors meant that consumers had more to consider than ever before and quick sales became less frequent.

By the start of 2000, the math had changed dramatically. In order for most dealers to sell a car, it took six to eight people to walk onto the lot. Sharp auto dealers realized there was a new set of math to prove and new sales methodologies to be created. But some dinosaurs, in an effort to hold on to the historically proven math, turned up the heat and made their TO system harder and harder. These are the people with the horrible reputations, the bad customer satisfaction scores, and the same bad apples who the manufacturers are working aggressively to remove as franchised dealers. They had failed to prove the new math.

SOMEONE ELSE CAN PROVE THE MATH FOR YOU, BUT . . .

Owners or executives can put others in charge of proving the math, provided they're prepared to accept the outcomes as truth. That requires a lot of trust. Alternatively, proving the math can be assigned to several people or teams working independently of one another. That requires being prepared to accept the proven math of one person/team and lose the others.

Whoever proves the math becomes the de facto leader with sufficient credentials to launch a crusade. If you want to lead a fast business, first prove the math and then employ people who accept the proven math as the template for success. Then stop wasting time debating the merits of the math—just do it.

[A SIXTY-SECOND HEADS-UP]

- Everyone has an opinion about everything. Most opinions are speed bumps. The only valid opinions come from those who have proven the math.

- Without proving the math, most businesspeople pencil themselves into oblivion.

- Proving the math is an ongoing process.

- He or she who proves the math earns the right to lead.

- A business dealing with proven math doesn't waste time constantly trying to reinvent the wheel.

BE RUTHLESS WITH RESOURCES

*B*oo.com should be the poster child for the big dot.com fizzle. Boo.com began as a typical Web fairy tale. Ernst Malmsten (once called "a literary rock star" by *Elle* magazine) and his co-founder Kajsa Leander (a former model) had visions of an online store for designer sportswear with lots of high-fashion merchandise and features. They saw users spinning three-dimensional pictures of items and zooming in. They saw a "try-on" feature where a virtual paper doll let buyers see how a top and bottom would look together. Most of all, they saw themselves as the visionaries who created "the first truly cool e-tailer, with worldwide sales, marketing, and distribution capabilities."

Confusing haste with speed, six months after Ernst and Co. launched this heavily anticipated and publicized site, it sputtered, heaved, and then fell into insolvency. The people behind Boo.com burned through a £70 million war chest (about $108.7 million U.S.

dollars) in less than six months. Their torrential spending generated heaps of buzz and next to nothing in repeat customers or sustained business momentum. In fact, they generated so little goodwill that the ashes of Boo.com were picked up by Bright Station PLC for £250,000 (or $372,800) on May 31, 2000.

In retrospect, Mr. Malmsten said, "My mistake was not to have a counterpart who was a strong financial controller." This scene is playing out at dot com firms all over the Internet. These folks have collectively squandered more resources than the spoiled heirs of the biggest family fortunes. They have had no conscience about inefficient and ineffective spending. And supposed seasoned investment managers have given away their hard-earned resources and their investors' money to these unproven and careless people.

Achieving and maintaining speed is best achieved by people who have learned that as tough as it is, you have to be ruthless with resources. Every cracker has to be worried over as if it were your last or you won't be around long enough to worry about being fast.

OSCAR WILDE HAD IT RIGHT

Being ruthless with resources doesn't mean being cheap. Wilde said, "A cynic knows the price of everything and the value of nothing."

Frugal people like Steve Case, Lowry Mays, Leo Pujals, Stefan Persson, and the other fast businesspeople profiled in this book have been able to maintain momentum by being frugal and refusing to waste a nickel on anything that doesn't move their organizations forward in an opportunistic fashion. First-time visitors to Lowry Mays's Clear Channel Communications in San Antonio,

Texas, expecting to find the trappings of a huge media and entertainment company, will be disappointed. Waving his arms to display the space, son Randall, the CFO, asks, "Does this look like the headquarters of a $50 billion company?" It doesn't.

The sixth-floor space Clear Channel shares with other tenants is so jammed to the rafters with files, boxes, papers, legal briefs, memos, and previous years' budgets and reports that there's no place to sit down. In fact, there's so little space available that if the one conference room is in use, Lowry is frequently asked to vacate his office so that it can be used for a meeting. The small handful of executives and assistants who power this $50 billion dollar machine do so from miniscule offices and cubicles.

Not only are the Mays family and those who work around them oblivious to the lack of comfort and pizzazz, they seem to relish it. Truly fast companies have neither the time nor the inclination to allocate resources for anything other than that which will keep them fast. There are three principles we uncovered that help businesses to be ruthless with resources.

I. CREATIVE DESTRUCTION MAKES BUSINESS FAST

Remember a CEO named Al Dunlop? He got famous for remaking Scott Paper in the mid-1990s. Promoting "the absolute importance" of the shareholder, he fired 11,000 employees, sold off several business, and tripled Scott Paper's market value in a lightening fast 20 months. Along the way he got a nickname (Chainsaw) and became the hero of executives who wanted a fast track to shareholder growth.

A lot of business thinkers had been horrified by Dunlop's disregard for modern management concepts like quality circles, participative management, "open-source" innovation, and other kinds of modern business practices.

We felt the same . . . until we started researching this book. Now we've come to recognize that a lot of the momentum that drives companies to new heights starts with "chainsaw" decisions.

At General Electric, Jack Welch's relentless demand for efficient use of resources got him the nickname Neutron Jack. But after the dust settled, what GE has become is now a story that everybody wants to study. Sales have grown 370 percent and profits 570 percent. GE tops a lot of lists as the world's most admired company, and Welch has created more shareholder wealth than any CEO in history.

GE efficiency has upended a lot of conventional wisdom. (Like the idea that it takes one dollar of investment to get a dollar of increased capacity. Now at GE Lighting in Europe it takes just 12.5 cents.) GE has learned how to leverage fresh ideas and be ruthless with new spending. You'd have to be blind not to connect Jack Welch's "neutron" hits with the vitality of the company.

Joseph Schumpeter, an early twentieth-century economist and social thinker, introduced the concept of creative destruction. He used it to describe how innovation demolished the old and how the destruction of what exists leads to new patterns of growth in economies. We think it additionally explains why drastic resource reduction prompts surprisingly good transformations and speed.

When Lou Gerstner came to IBM, he forced sweeping reductions at the Nobel Prize–winning IBM Research Division. Head counts dropped 28 percent as the division attempted to live with budgets that were shrunk 37 percent based on 1990 levels. One physicist grumbled, "All the infrastructure I had built up over fifteen years was destroyed. The long-term outlook went very sour."

But from the attic cleaning and deep-cavity probes this "destruction" created an energized staff and customer-focused research into areas of real commercial value. Today, the pace of breakthroughs has quickened spectacularly. Said research director Paul Horn, "Now winning is taking ideas . . . and being *the fastest* in converting them into a significant technological advantage."

Have you ever worked for someone with impossible deadlines? Have you ever been forced to make due with a lot less than your competition? Have you seen the better productivity that follows a comprehensive reduction in personnel? Have you ever started a business by mortgaging everything and living on your credit cards? How many invaluable lessons did you learn? And how did the experiences change your thinking and behavior? The pressure of deep cuts and a scramble for resources brings original views and clever solutions. And the urgency it creates is fundamental to achieving fast change.

2. TIME AND KNOWLEDGE ARE THE CRITICAL RESOURCES FOR THE TWENTY-FIRST CENTURY

Last century's management was obsessed with one resource of an organization—money. They counted paperclips, beat up suppliers to get the lowest price, and used their profits and losses as a guideline for every decision. That worked well to a point . . . as markets were stable, employees were interchangeable, and change came in years instead of weeks.

But since the mid-1980s, traditional asset manipulators and cost controllers produced a terrible track record. The results of that traditional management produced an average growth rate of just 1.4 percent. (Standard and Poor's 500 average growth rate adjusted for inflation between 1984 and 1994). In fact, among the nation's 1,000 largest companies, only 7 percent of profitable growers between 1988 and 1993 were cost cutters in the previous five years according to a Mercer Management Consulting study. In contrast, revenue growers have seen their shareholder value increase 25 percent per year over the same period.

Who are these fast revenue growers? Home Depot, Dell, Intel, The Gap, and GE, among others, are highly successful examples of firms that prospered from 1985 to 1995. Following them in the 1990s were AOL, Charles Schwab, H&M, Clear Channel Communications, Lend Lease, Telepizza, and others whose stories we tell. AOL didn't exist before 1985 and today has a greater market value than Ford and General Motors combined. Leo Pujals turned a $100,000 investment into a company valued at $2 billion, Schwab became the largest financial services firm on the planet, and Clear Channel became the world's largest out-of-home media company. Time and knowledge and the judicious allocation of financial resources are what led to these remarkable revenue growths.

Ruthless use of time and demands to do it quicker and better separate the winners from the losers. H&M has taken the time from design idea to finished goods in 800 stores from twelve months to three months. They manage to cut time as well as costs. Charles Schwab introduced seamless trading on the Internet within months of conception. Hotmail took an idea to the marketplace with only $300,000 in funding.

Knowledge includes all the valuable concepts and vital know-how that shape a business to be wanted and needed by customers. Companies that are fast to market and have demonstrated an ability to sustain speed view time and knowledge as assets that are as real as money in the bank.

3. FIRST THINGS FIRST AND SECOND THINGS . . . NOT AT ALL

Deciding what tasks deserve resources and what tasks don't are some of the toughest choices in management. Some allocate their time, money, and knowledge to whatever is in their face. For them, the squeaky wheel gets the grease. Others are democratic—if ten tasks present themselves, each gets 10 percent of the available resources. But leaders with a track record of fast action have learned to set priorities based on an old maxim called Pareto's principle.

Vilfredo Pareto lived in the nineteenth century. Trained in both the French and Italian schools, he was an engineer who made a unique contribution to economics. One of his conclusions was that concentration is the natural pattern of distribution in economics. This was labeled the 80/20 formula, or Pareto's principle.

Pareto's principle teaches us that 20 percent of the items for sale in a business generate 80 percent of the revenues, or that 80 percent of what you sell will contribute only 20 percent of profits. That is, 80 percent of what most people decide to do is only good for the other 20 percent of the results. This explains why across-the-board cost cuts don't add but a few last gasps to a business when it is circling the drain. The cuts are never deep enough to get rid of the real waste, and across-the-board cuts take resources away from the few things that are making a big contribution.

Ruthlessness starts with a cold, hard analysis of what's important and what's not. And then you have to choose what is likely to yield the most results and do that first, leaving the rest to solve itself or go undone.

CHALLENGE EVERY DOLLAR SPENT EVERY TIME

Each year, the general managers of each Clear Channel radio station, television station, and outdoor company put together a twelve-month budget and plan of action for their business units. Then they sit down with Mark, Randall, and Lowry and pitch the plan. Clear Channel managers can propose anything in their budget that makes sense from their perspective. If they want to change formats, increase staff size, change commission structures, or move into a new facility, everything's up to them except two things.

The Clear Channel commandments are that cash flow must increase every year and every year's budget begins at zero. Just because money was allocated to something the previous year doesn't automatically mean it will be spent again. To drive home the point, Clear Channel's managers are paid on increased cash flow.

Most Clear Channel managers say with a wink and feigning physical infirmity that budget sessions with Mark, Randall, and Lowry are the same as having someone walk up and down your back with football spikes. Mark Mays agrees the process is a tough one for everyone involved: "Of course it's a strenuous process. Every revenue objective and expense is challenged. We ask questions about *every* single line in the budget." With an inimitable and diabolical grin, he adds, "And ... if ... something seems amiss ... we get into it ... in even greater ... detail."

Mays says the only objective is to achieve or exceed the plan: "We don't put a goal out there for them not to achieve it. All our managers are compensated on growing their cash flow each year. It's all very simple. Our stock price increases because our cash flow increases. Our cash flow grows because of increased operating expenses."

Any business—whether the local tire shop or IBM—wishing to be fast and opportunistic must remain constantly vigilant about the allocation of resources.

[A SIXTY-SECOND HEADS-UP] ➡

- Make sure you know the difference between frugal and cheap, and then be frugal.
- Three principles for being ruthless with resources:
    1. Creative destruction can make businesses fast.
    2. Time and knowledge are the critical resources for the twenty-first century.
    3. First things first and second things... not at all.
- Challenge every dollar spent.

USE A CENTRAL SCOREBOARD

All businesses have scoreboards. Given current technology, there's probably not a manager left who is unable, with a simple point and click, to retrieve constantly updated reports on sales, accounts receivable and payable, cost of goods sold, personnel records, returned merchandise, and gross profit . . . ad infinitum.

But when it's all been said and done, the scoreboards of most companies are designed to measure one thing—profits. If sales aren't up to scratch, most managers go and pound on the salespeople. Maybe they need a motivational pep talk. If costs are too high, they either direct a few bodies to be off-loaded or advertising expenditures to be cut. And, if there are too many product returns of faulty merchandise, they beat up on the plant manager or threaten a supplier.

We discovered a major difference between the centralized scoreboards of companies that have demonstrated the ability to maintain speed and their slower-moving competitors.

EVERYONE MEASURES AND SCORES WHAT'S REALLY IMPORTANT TO THEM

Everybody measures what's personally important. Most people keep a relatively accurate account of their checking, savings, and investment balances because money is important to them. Despite their protestation that it's just a pinch of this and a bit of that, good cooks measure ingredients because an appetizing finished product is important to them. And good parents measure the whereabouts, progress, and activities of their children because their kids are important to them.

When the ultimate measurement on a company scoreboard is profit, the company has announced that profit is the most important thing. Unfortunately, when profit becomes the exclusive aim of an organization, people within the company find themselves ready to embrace almost any tactic to achieve it. Often, the selection of inappropriate tactics, which frequently require being unwound and tried again, proves to be very shortsighted. Profit actually becomes elusive.

COMPANIES THAT STAY FAST MEASURE ACTIVITY

The Clear Channel central scoreboard is at corporate headquarters in San Antonio, Texas, where the company takes every annual operating plan and breaks it down into the smallest activity-based component parts. If, as a result of the annual planning session between the station's general manager and the Mays family, the station's total revenues objective for the year is $12 million, with half of that representing free cash flow, the scoreboard—which is updated weekly—

does not measure the big number being chased but the activities that will allow the big number to be achieved.

If the general manager's plan called for the $12 million to be achieved by having eighteen local salespeople on the streets, each making five sales daily, the Clear Channel scoreboard tracks how many salespeople are on staff and how many sales calls were actually made. Because of Clear Channel's central scorekeeping, they know not only how many salespeople are on the streets selling advertising and how much they're selling but the average rate a commercial or billboard is being sold for, the percentage of inventory utilized, and by whom. At the first sign of a minute variance from the agreed plan, the general managers know they'll receive a telephone call of inquiry. Instead of offering a weak excuse, they'd better be prepared with an explanation of how the variance has already been corrected.

Clear Channel understands that the total is the sum of the parts, and that if people are only shooting at the big number, they'll do some strange things to achieve it. By keeping everyone focused on and constantly measuring the smallest activity-based component of the plan, they know the big number will be achieved.

Some people might think that measuring and scoring every operational detail smacks of a lack of trust. That's not what we uncovered. We found employees, staff, and executives who relish having their every activity monitored and scored because they understand they're part of fast-moving teams that have big goals to score and games to win.

Leo Pujals frequently compares business to sports when he shares his view on the need to measure and score everything: "Here in Spain, people go and play sports and have fun. Then they go to work and are unhappy because it's something they have to do. Scoring puts fun and competitiveness into business."

Pujals asks, "Can you imagine sitting in a gymnasium and watching a basketball game where no score was kept? It would be boring watching people go up and down the floor shooting baskets with no idea of who was winning and who was losing."

Pujals insists that keeping close score not only puts fun into the business but also provides invaluable information that allows for fast corrective action to be taken. Each day at Telepizza, headquarters company leaders review comprehensive printouts of the previous day's activities. If enough fliers weren't delivered or enough extra cheese on pizzas and orders of garlic bread weren't sold, the Telepizza equivalent of a SWAT team swoops in and immediately fixes the activity problem. Leo Pujals says managing a company of 1,000 restaurants is easy: "Even a monkey can make good decisions if it has all the facts."

Business leaders who want their enterprise to stay fast break down the big number into bite-sized activity-based pieces and measure and score the achievement of the activities.

[A SIXTY-SECOND HEADS-UP] ➡

- Most companies keep track of the dollars. Companies that are consistently fast monitor and score the activities that create the dollars.

- When only the final financial result counts as a score on the board, people are likely to embrace any tactic to achieve the big number.

- Measuring and scoring activity allows companies to take immediate corrective action.

STAY FINANCIALLY FLEXIBLE

In the 1980s, conventional wisdom was that you could borrow your way to a business fortune. Junk bonds, bank debt, and fast public offerings provided the quick answer for building business wealth, and guys like Donald Trump and Michael Milliken were leading the way. Some of these leveraged deals worked out well. But a lot of easy debt didn't. By overpaying for real estate, company acquisitions, and IPOs (initial public offerings), many "smart" people made themselves poorer.

Even some of the winners of the leverage game have to question the tactic today. Craig McCaw (one of our heroes) took $250 million plus $5 billion in debt and turned it into the first nationwide cellular network. But later, pinched by the debt burden, McCaw sold the whole thing to AT&T for $11.5 billion. It might seem like a leverage success story. After all, McCaw netted about $800 million for himself. But last March, when AT&T sold a chunk of

McCaw's old network in an IPO for $73 billion (a sixfold return in just seven years), Craig McCaw must have wished he'd maintained greater flexibility in the early 1990s and held on to his network.

One player who decided not to play the leverage game during the 1980s was the Mays family and Clear Channel Communications. "When everybody else [in radio] was bidding up the prices of stations and leveraging themselves to the hilt, we said, 'Whoa, this is crazy'; it doesn't fit our criteria," says Randall Mays. "We decided we should sit on the sidelines."

From those sidelines, Clear Channel perfected their model of running a media property like a business: using decentralized management, grinding out lots of efficiencies, and maintaining constant vigilance on all financial issues. The Mays family saw the 1980s close with hundreds of leveraged stations in trouble and banks willing to do deals with someone with a strong balance sheet. Clear Channel Communications then had their pick of the best radio station buys.

Continuing to emphasize cash flow performance and strong balance sheet flexibility, Clear Channel impressed both banks and the share market. Their high-stock multiple and great reputation for hitting cash flow forecast made them even more able to take their pick of the deals. Staying financially flexible, which allowed them to be opportunistic, is credited by the founders as the best decisions they ever made.

Financial flexibility provides a lot of advantages:

- You earn flexibility by keeping bankers and other finance experts out of the decision-making process.

- You have quick cash on hand to jump on a major opportunity.

- You have shareholders who are looking at a long-term payoff rather than next quarter's dividend.

- You have time on your side.

Financial flexibility is just the beginning at companies like Clear Channel, Charles Schwab, H&M, AOL, and others. In fact, these companies and others like them have made *staying flexible* key to every decision. For example, Charles Schwab saw the rising tide of common individuals ready to own stocks and mutual funds. But Schwab also saw the thousands of independent financial planners, regional brokers, and banks all over the nation who'd benefit from using Schwab's technology. Rather than lock them out and treat them like despised competitors, Schwab made them into customers too. Schwab reached out to these independents and tailored services to meet their needs and build on their independence. Those partnerships today are responsible for nearly 40 percent of Schwab's management assets. Schwab was flexible about who could be a customer.

Clear Channel was flexible about the entire model of local media management. Recognizing that the key to success in many other industries was spreading management expenses over much larger activity centers, Clear Channel took eight separate radio operations and brought them all under one general and administrative staff and budget. Then, seeing that local decision making would give them the fastest and most accountable business units, they refused to add any management above the local operating unit and kept headquarters staffing low—all in contrast to the other players in media.

H&M saw that if they were to turn stock eight times yearly (double the traditional clothing retailer) they had to drive down prices on fashionable items to levels below the discount merchants. They developed in-house brands, sourced their own manufacturing, found alternatives in fabric and design, and delivered goods that were both chic and priced to move *fast*. They were flexible about what the customer would and would not accept in getting fashion at low prices. With $19 bikinis and $25 black crochet dresses, H&M's basic shopping basket is 45 percent less expensive than The Gap.

The hallmark of success in dealing with the speed of markets and opportunities is maintaining flexibility. You can't let yourself be tied to conventional wisdom or traditions. Flexibility means throwing out old assumptions and constantly rearranging the pieces of the business to get the best results.

> *Men are born soft and supple;*
> *dead, they are stiff and hard.*
> *Plants are born tender and pliant;*
> *Dead, they are brittle and dry.*
> *Thus, whoever is stiff and inflexible*
> *is a disciple of death.*
> *Whoever is soft and yielding*
> *is a disciple of life.*
> —The Tao Te Ching

SURVIVAL OF THE MOST ADAPTIVE

Henry Ford wrote, "Businesses that grow by development and improvement do not die. But when a business ceases to be creative, when it believes it has reached perfection and needs to do nothing but produce—it is done." What makes those great words even more interesting is that when Ford himself was faced with a slowdown in the popularity of his famous Model T, instead of following his own advice, he decreed the only thing that was wrong was that the sales-people weren't producing enough and needed to work harder. The old man obviously believed his Model T was "perfection" and all Ford Motors needed to do was produce. This turns out to be a more common attitude among one-time innovators than business lore would make you believe.

The most famous innovator of the late 1800s had to be Thomas Edison. The motion picture, stock ticker, phonograph, electric lamp—over 1,043 patents were held by the "Wizard of Menlo Park." Yet by 1889, the man who was once a bold and courageous innovator turned into an arch obstructer and defender of the status quo. His efforts to thwart alternating current (as a competitor to his direct current methods) led him to help New York State execute criminals using an electric chair powered by alternating current. His hope was to scare the public out of any interest in alternating current for the home or business by making it appear dangerous and lethal. Edison—the captain of innovation—had become as hard and inflexible as those he had earlier railed against.

Think about some of the opportunities that some of the best in the business have blown:

- Dell's direct sales model was available to IBM, Compaq, HP, and even Apple. Where was their flexibility?

- Schwab's discount brokerage idea was open to Merrill Lynch, Smith Barney, and the rest who said, "It'll never amount to anything."

- The Big Three Networks all had divisions running radio stations. What kept them from doing what Clear Channel has done?

Almost every major advance in commerce was made right under the nose of the most successful people in the business:

- GE and Westinghouse had fluorescent lighting. But they let little Sylvania, a fringe producer, lead in the sales and capture a 20 percent share of the growing market.

- RCA had the transistor but let Texas Instruments, Fairchild, and Motorola win 42 percent of the market.

- Only one department store chain harnessed the power of discount stores (Dayton Hudson's Target Division).

- Wal-Mart even took the original Sears crusade, "To give ordinary folk the chance to buy the same things as rich people," and outdid Sears.

Years ago, Prodigy, at that time the biggest name in the Internet, saw that their customers were using more and more e-mail. This strained their internal systems and created difficulties for the systems resources. "Enough is enough," harrumphed one boss. So the executives at Prodigy slapped a surcharge of 25 cents for every e-mail over thirty per month that a user tried to send. They must have thought that surcharges would get their customers to be more reasonable with their e-mail usage or at least Prodigy would be profiting. *An archenemy of speed is a lack of flexibility.*

[A SIXTY-SECOND HEADS-UP]

- It isn't the strongest of the species that survives—it's the most flexible.

- Financial flexibility allows a company to be opportunistic.

- Flexible thinking allows companies to recognize new groups of customers.

- Nothing fails like success. Most successful companies become so locked into their way of doing business that they refuse to acknowledge new ways.

USE NARRATIVES AND STORIES

One of the challenges facing businesses hoping to maintain momentum is keeping everyone with the organization firmly committed to being fast.

- New people joining the enterprise must be brought quickly up to speed.
- The existing personnel mustn't be allowed to lose their passion for speed.

Unfortunately, the orientation at most companies is limited to, "Here are some forms to fill out, HR has a video everyone has to see, then they'll give you a tour and show you around, the boss wanted to buy you lunch, but she's out of town, so take a day and settle in . . . let me know if you need anything . . . *the end*."

CALL SOMEONE A HORSE TEN TIMES...
THEY'LL START LOOKING FOR HAY.

CALL THEM FAST TEN TIMES...THEY'LL START BELIEVING IT.

One discovery we made while studying fast companies surprised and delighted us: fast companies have institutionalized the telling of stories to ensure that new people joining the company are quickly brought into and made part of the fast culture. What makes storytelling its own virtuous circle is that not only do the stories serve to teach new hires, but, in the telling of their stories, the storytellers are staking out a position they'll be required to live up to in the future.

Schwab co-CEO Dave Pottruck embraces storytelling as a tactic for staying fast to market. "Because of our fast growth, each time we have a management meeting at least 20 percent of the people are newly promoted or new to the company, and it's our obligation to get them up to speed as fast as possible." Pottruck explains his tactic this way:

> When we have a meeting we go as far as erecting a stage with a fireplace and a rocking chair and after dinner we announce, "Tonight is story night," and everyone takes their turn on stage telling their personal Schwab stories that epitomize who we are, our values, our cause, our guiding principles, where we're going, and how fast we're going to get there.

STORIES MAKE THE IDEOLOGY COME ALIVE

Every business has an ethos. Unfortunately, most companies that decide on a set of values or ethics publish them once and consider the job done. Regular exposure to the stories of an organization not only ensures that everyone gets up to speed fast but that the listener has a sense of the job being more than a job. People imagine themselves as part of the stories and endeavor to create their own that tell their personal story of the firm's ideologies.

In *Leading Minds, An Anatomy of Leadership*, Professor Howard Gardner of Harvard University presents a compelling case for the use of stories:

> In recent years social scientists have come to appreciate what political, religious and military figures have long known; that stories, narratives, myths and fables constitute a uniquely powerful currency in human relationships. And, I suggest further, that it's stories of identity, narratives that help individuals think and feel about who they are, where they come from and where they're headed, that constitute the single most powerful weapon in the leader's arsenal.

An integral part of the interviewing process at Telepizza during the reign of Leo Pujals was the Telepizza stories, which ended with an invitation to join the company and become a Telepizza citizen. Leo Pujals credits storytelling as being his secret weapon for finding and keeping good people:

> The only reasons we've been able to move fast and maintain our incredible speed are the people who work with me and share my dream. The Romans had a culture, and whether they were in Iberia, Cairo, or Alexander, Romans were proud citizens of Rome. My dream was to turn everyone we hired into a Telepizza citizen,

someone sharing the same knowledge, values, truths, and commitment to moving fast.

So important was storytelling to the fast roll out of Telepizza that Pujals even made stories a key ingredient in the road shows done for potential investors. "Here, look at the picture of this man, he beams like a proud father, this is Eduardo Hernandez. He finished law school while working for us as a delivery boy and went up the ladder to assistant store manager, store manager, supervisor, sales manager, and today he runs Portugal."

Being frugal is one of the key guiding principles at Clear Channel Communications, and while it's one thing to proclaim a value, it's another to illustrate the point with institutionalized stories about billionaire Lowry Mays driving an old Willy jeep that's falling apart and wearing the same pair of trademark khakis and shirt for a week when he's at his ranch. All Clear Channel conferences feature stories and anecdotes told by his sons attesting to the thrift and frugality of their father. Then Lowry takes the stage and in a homespun and credible way he talks at length about the Clear Channel story, the humble origins of the company, the values it stands for, and the importance of rewarding the shareholders who have invested their economic futures in the firm. Even people who have been with the company since its beginning sit rapt with attention, and more than a few moist eyes are seen round the room as some of the same stories are told over and over again. Repeated exposure ensures that everyone gets and understands the Clear Channel message.

Storytelling was the only currency Sabeer Bhatia had to convince people to give up their jobs and join him in pursuit of a dream. At Lend Lease, staff and executive gatherings seem more like Amway rallies than serious business sessions, with more time devoted to the telling of Lend Lease stories than routine business. Steve Case used stories and myths about what could be to entice more than eighty CEOs to trade their companies for AOL stock.

EVERY BUSINESS HAS STORIES

But people forget to tell stories or only the important people get to hear them. In order for storytelling to be an effective tactic, stories must be institutionalized and integrated into the orientation of every new staff member and told regularly for the benefit of everyone. Leaders must decide which stories and anecdotes convey the intended message and then create regular forums where they'll be told and heard. While storytelling must begin with the leader, the tactic becomes even more effective when others are invited to join in—à la Schwab—and tell their stories of the company. If speed is the objective, then it's stories of speed and fast to market that must be told and celebrated.

[A SIXTY-SECOND HEADS-UP] ➡

- In order to maintain speed, a business needs to ensure that new staff members get up to speed as quickly as possible.
- Stories, narratives, myths, and fables are a leader's most important currency.
- Stories let people know who they are, where they're going, and why.

- To serve as an effective tactic, storytelling must become institutionalized.
- List your business's great stories that reflect where your company is headed.

  1. _____

  2. _____

  3. _____

  4. _____

  5. _____

PLAY YOUR OWN GAME

One of the speed bumps that slows down businesses is paying undue attention to the competition and what they're up to. "Did you see what the competition announced yesterday? Let's call a meeting." *Thwack.* "Did you see their earnings? What in the hell will we say about ours?" *Thwack, thwack.* "I bet our market share is still higher than theirs. We should do some focus groups with their customers." *Thwack, thwack, thwack.*

Every moment invested in thinking about, analyzing, and attempting to explain the success or failure of a competitor is time that could have been spent being faster. If a competitor is doing well, it'll make you envious and defensive about what you do. If a competitor is doing poorly and that's how you get your jollies, you have an empty life, your preoccupations are misplaced, and we're happy not to be your shareholders.

FORGET ABOUT THE COMPETITION

The fastest companies in the world don't give the competition a passing thought. Dave Pottruck of Schwab sums up his company's attitude about the competition this way: "In all my time with Schwab, I'm unaware of Chuck Schwab ever having paid any attention to the competition. Chuck Schwab simply isn't interested in whatever anyone else is doing. He only cares about what we're doing for our customers."

Mark and Randall Mays of Clear Channel Communications share the same feelings:

> We just don't spend time thinking or talking about what the competition is doing; it only slows you down. We run a simple business; we pay attention to the basics like blocking, tackling, increasing revenues, controlling expenses, increasing shareholder value, all of which allow us to be opportunistic. It's much more rewarding to be in a position to buy the competition than to spend time changing your game plan to match theirs.

There's never been a more beleaguered business leader than Steve Case of AOL. Attacked relentlessly by the high-tech press, one Silicon Valley magazine went so far as to publish a photo of Case's head atop a maid's uniform carrying a vacuum cleaner with a huge headline asking, "Does AOL Suck?" David Hilzenrath of the *Washington Post* labeled Case and AOL "the splendid coach that had turned into a pumpkin"; and Ann Winblad, a revered Venture capitalist from Silicon Valley, parried that, "AOL had lost the cachet required to attract consumers who want the latest hot, cool thing." Even some of Case's fellow board members wanted to sell the company to Microsoft for peanuts, with former Secretary of State Al Haig whining, "We'll never be able to beat Prodigy or CompuServe."

A lesser leader would have caved in and changed strategy. Case refused to bend and continued to play his own game, proving the math, acquiring subscribers by the millions, with scant regard for what the competition was doing.

When we asked H&M's Fabian Mansson to compare his company's financial performance to The Gap's, he was incredulous and offended:

> "How would we know what The Gap is doing and why would we care? We run our own game and try to do it faster every day than the day before. It's fashion, quality, and price and doing it fast. Why would we allow ourselves to become preoccupied with another fashion retailer? It would cause us to take our eye off the ball."

Stuart Hornery, chair of Lend Lease, seemed genuinely amused when we asked him to compare his company to the competition:

> We don't spend much time worrying about our competitors. We wish them well and hope everything goes fine for them. We do our thing and spend all our time trying to do it better, building things of value and beauty that have never been built, positively impacting the lives of our associates and shareholders, and working hard to be responsible citizens. We don't have time to worry about the competition.

Leo Pujals of Telepizza believes his competition went upside down because they spent too much time studying Telepizza. "Pizza Hut went bankrupt here in Spain, and it happened for two reasons: they spent all their time studying us and trying to figure out what we were doing and they wore suits. Who in the hell wears suits in the pizza business?"

WE DON'T SUCK WORSE THAN THEM

At most company headquarters, armies of analysts, planners, and mangers spend their days trotting out reams of reports and statistics so that their bosses can prove to the board of directors, "Here, look at this . . . we're no worse off than our competition. Can I keep my job please?"

Any business that spends an appreciable amount of time studying the competition won't have time to be fast or to be a trailblazer and will be relegated to traveling ground that's been trod before. Innovation and being fast to market comes from studying customers—not competitors—and then playing your own game.

[**A SIXTY-SECOND HEADS-UP**] ➡

- Most companies spend a disproportionate share of resources comparing themselves to their competitors.
- The fastest businesses on the planet assiduously avoid such wasted effort and concentrate on their enterprises.
- Most time spent studying other businesses isn't intelligence gathering as much as a search for excuses.

DON'T B.S. YOURSELF

*P*reviously we related the story of the wizened entrepreneur who advised us early in our careers that, "Sometimes you may have to B.S. the customer, sometimes you may have to B.S. the employees, . . . but don't ever think that means it's okay to B.S. yourself. Believing your own PR sets you up for failure."

Leaders who want to keep their business moving at top speed set up organizations that don't B.S. themselves. GE has sustained high speed for almost two decades. While experts point to many reasons, Jack Welch says it's GE's informality that leads to their in-your-face, just-do-it culture. By informality he means an environment where no one is afraid to tell the boss he's all wet.

At GE everyone is committed to workouts. Workouts are meetings that can be called by anybody to address any problem, large or small, with no bosses in attendance. After the participants have a plan—for example, how to kill a useless form or how to change a balky process—the boss is informed, "We had a workout and need to talk to you." He or she must then make a decision on the spot. There can be no haggling or delays even though the manager knows nothing is being questioned until someone says, "Let me tell you about the workout we just had."

Workouts let GE up-end traditional executive power and allow people to push back at the bosses. Says Welch, "Getting a company to be informal is a huge deal."

The U.S. Army also has institutionalized a no-B.S. approach to leadership. Take a look at how they talk to the newest generals at the army's Brigadier General Training Conference: "Each and every one of you has something that makes you a jerk. Some of you have more than one. I know. I've talked to you. And if you don't believe me . . . ask your spouses. They're dying to tell you."

The army knows rank may have its privileges, but it also has its traps. And the fawning and flattery that accompany promotions lead to arrogant management and flawed decision making. So they teach the baby generals to get in touch with their inner jerk. They know there is no payoff from letting leaders B.S. themselves.

How can you avoid buying your own B.S.?

- Ruthlessly track intentions and outcomes.

- Ruthlessly control delusions of grandeur.

- Ruthlessly collect disconfirming evidence.

RUTHLESSLY TRACK INTENTIONS AND OUTCOMES

Can you imagine starting out on a vacation without a destination? Without a destination, you can't plan how to get there or budget or make any other decision. But a lot of management happens without a really clear idea of where we expect to be after the decision is made. That is partly the fault of the new demand for speed in business. The nature of management's work now is to make hundreds of decisions every day. And the pace of competition forces us to do all our deciding on the run. So we feel rushed into adopting a "ready . . . fire . . . aim" mentality. And that's not all bad.

Percy Barnevik of ASEA Brown Boveri has a rule of thumb for the evaluation of his managers. He encourages them to make decisions quickly, arguing that an imperfect decision made on Monday that can be adjusted is far better than a painstakingly accurate decision made a week later. His rule of 7–3 says that out of ten decisions, an executive only has to be right seven times, and he or she will still be far better than a slower-moving counterpart. But even under the rule of 7–3, you need clear destinations to be embedded in every decision.

Deeper down exists another motivation for a manager's failure to always have explicit intentions before taking off in a direction. Managers are nervous about exposing inabilities and incompetence. They know that every stated intention sets up a benchmark against which their decision making can be measured. They suspect what studies since 1984 have concluded: half of all decisions in business fail to achieve the stated objective. (Dr. Paul C. Nutt, professor of management at Ohio State University, reporting to the Academy of Management Executives on studies completed for *Administrative Science Quarterly, Academy of Management Journal,* and *Organization Science.)*

To avoid facing this unpleasant truth, managers are systematically vague in their goals and intentions. Uncertainty makes management intentionally fuzzy. To say, "We must satisfy our customers," is a lot easier than deciding what *to do* and what *not* to do and then measuring satisfaction scientifically. And being vague avoids all accountability.

To suggest the facility should be user-friendly is much quicker than figuring out what users want and how it can pay off. And it is never really clear if you were successful. When goals and intentions are clearly stated and communicated, there is no room for B.S. This record of intentions is like a scorecard that shows the strengths and weaknesses of the manager's game.

RUTHLESSLY CONTROL DELUSIONS OF GRANDEUR

Taking command in today's business we see executives who crave new experiences and daring challenges. Steve Case of AOL, Charles Schwab and Dave Pottruck of Charles Schwab, Lowry Mays of Clear Channel, Stefan Persson of H&M are right alongside Andy Grove, Jeff Bezos, Steve Jobs, Jack Welch, and a long list of familiar names as leaders whose high profiles shape their companies and the world.

To Sigmund Freud, these and many other leaders today share a personality type he dubbed "narcissistic" (from the Greek figure Narcissus, who dies because of an overwhelming preoccupation with himself). Freud wrote: "People of this type impress others as being 'personalities.' They are especially suited to take on the role as leaders."

Narcissistic personalities have performed spectacularly throughout history. They have inspired entire nations (for example, Gandhi, Roosevelt, and Churchill) and led the way to new and exciting business futures (for example, Edison, Ford, and Morita). But there is a dark side too. Great leaders can let their achievements feed delusions of omnipotence, and their strong sense of purpose can feed irrational obstinacy and thin-skinned rages.

On the downside, Freud taught that narcissists don't generally like give and take with others. They are often very sensitive to snubs and bruise as easily as a peach. They therefore like to take over meetings, pursue doctrine over debate, and can be shockingly harsh with anyone around them who expresses doubt or contrary conclusions. As one executive at Oracle said of boss Larry Ellison, "The difference between God and Larry is that God doesn't believe He is Larry."

In order to keep a company moving fast, the trick is to harness the productive forces of the leadership personality without giving in to the dark side.

GET IN TOUCH WITH YOUR INNER JERK

The ability to deal with the causes of irrational and uncontrolled behavior is the difference between productive and destructive narcissism. You start by discovering that such defects exist. This can be done through formal talks with trained professionals (those who specialize in management psychology) or informally with those who know and love you (as the U.S. Army was doing when they asked the new generals to listen to their spouses and children).

Executives should put significant energy into the traits that neutralize a leader's traditional failings: greater self-reflection, more detachment and good humor, lots of empathetic listening, and practicing what you preach.

GET AN OFF-SIDER

Most managers are followed closely by a platoon of yes-men and office politicians. They tell managers what managers want to hear and work to keep all the bad news away. As one manager commented to us, "If our boss stops too fast, he'll find at least one of his favorite executive's heads up his butt."

The Australians have a tradition that executives should have a trusted sidekick who's allowed to "take the piss out of" the boss. This "off-sider" tethers the executive to reality and works to bring new ideas and essential criticism to the leader. It's sort of like the legendary position of fool or jester to a king. This is the one person who by contract or agreement is secure enough to push the leader into addressing his flaws and calming unproductive urges. Every leader needs an off-sider. Too much agreement is dangerous to mental health.

As the late Akiro Morita said after a dispute with the then chairperson of Sony: "Sir, if you and I had exactly the same ideas on all subjects, it would be unnecessary for both of us to be in this company. It is precisely because you and I have different ideas that this company will run a smaller risk of making mistakes."

RUTHLESSLY COLLECT DISCONFIRMING EVIDENCE

There is a clear connection between being a leader who can create a crusade and being a leader with a highly flawed memory. True believers, it seems, maintain terrible memory skills. Studies show they remember the facts that conflict with their beliefs only 40 percent of the time. Skeptics better that performance by more than double, remembering both confirming and disconfirming evidence 90 percent of the time.

Leaders rely on their memories when making fast decisions. And by a believer's nature, those memories lead managers to B.S. themselves. That means leaders need to work hard at collecting and remembering the facts that refute their impulses.

The army has created a great idea for getting disconfirming evidence front and center. It's called the after-action review (AAR). Following major exercises, a critique is held that includes representatives from all the ranks. In a completely free environment, all AAR participants tear into every decision by the hierarchy. Using data and facts rather than opinions, they look at what succeeded and failed and the reasons for both.

According to a former commander of the National Training Center, "The after-action review . . . resocialized officers to move away from a command and control style and move to a style that takes advantage of distributed intelligence. It has taught us never to become too wedded to our script and to remain versatile." The army has learned you can't B.S. yourself in an environment of straight talk.

To be able to maintain speed, every business needs its own version of the after-action review—one that asks intrusive questions of every level of the hierarchy, that forces managers to face and grade their assumptions, and that makes executives shuffle their portfolio of cherished ideas and sacred cows.

[**A SIXTY-SECOND HEADS-UP**]➡

- Don't B.S. yourself.
- Implement workout sessions in your business.
- Track intentions and outcomes.
- If successful, control your inevitable delusions of grandeur.
- Ruthlessly search for disconfirming evidence.

STAY CLOSE TO THE CUSTOMER

*T*here are no customers more fickle than kids. How to stay with, let alone ahead of, what's fresh and lame to teenagers and subteens is almost impossible. Take it from South Park's Eric Cartman. When his classmate Kyle showed up with what he thought was the coolest toy from the new Japanese craze Chimpokomon, Cartman sneered, "Oh Kyle . . . that is so last week!"

So we have been especially attentive whenever Tom Freston, CEO of MTV Networks, speaks. Over the last thirteen years, he has kept MTV, Nickelodeon, and VH1 consistently fresh . . . a worldwide trendsetter in the youth market. "I think if we can be totally connected with our viewers . . . and get inside their heads and their closets, their CD collections, and translate that along with a lot of internal intuition into a product, everything else in our business will fall into place." Freston credits his organization's success with young consumers to relentless research, a young staff that genuinely *like* their customers' tastes, and his understanding that the only thing constant in his business is change. That mirrors the views of the leadership at H&M, Clear Channel Communications, Charles Schwab, Telepizza, and AOL.

Finding, keeping, and growing the right customers requires knowing and *liking* the customers. But, like everything else that separates the fast from the slow, *that's* much more easily said than done. Why?

- Most businesses can't tell who is the "right" customer.

- Even when they have found the "right" customer, most businesses don't listen.

- And most of the time they don't like what they hear.

WHO IS THE RIGHT CUSTOMER?

The first hurdle for businesses looking to increase their internal clock speed is to get over the worst assumption in customer selection: "If you've got the money, we've got the time!" We spent years finding out the hard way that just because the customer can buy doesn't mean we should sell to them. The color green doesn't always mean go. The wrong customers can be an abomination.

MARGINAL BUYERS CAUSE EMPLOYEE AND GOOD CUSTOMER BURNOUT

The airlines offer the worst customer service experience in mass markets. They are the only stores on earth where you can spend thousands in full-fare purchases and still get treated like an annoyance. We used to think it was the result of unions and old-age employees. But it is likely that the too-good-to-be-true fares have brought in many of the worst customers on the planet. Inundated by a clientele that's pushy, overbearing, and cheap, it's no wonder that front-line employees have begun treating everyone like the lowest common denominator. The wrong customer reduces *both* employee and customer loyalty.

EVERY MARGINAL DEAL USES THE SAME, IF NOT *MORE*, FINANCIAL RESOURCES AS THE BEST-PAYING CUSTOMERS

Peter Drucker proved it years ago in *Managing for Results*. Being indiscriminate about what you sell and who you do business with wastes a business's most valuable resource—money available for opportunities. But the lure of incremental business (those orders you get after you reach break-even) has blinded many executives to the true expense of keeping and growing a customer. Companies end up pushing every day to get out of the holes they dug the day before.

Business thinking should always start with and constantly assess who the "right" customers are and what they value when they buy. This is most easily done by laying out the criteria for the wrong customer, such as:

- Needing too deep a discount, too many concessions, or impossible service levels

- Believing you and your competitors are all the same and showing no capacity for loyalty

- Behaving badly, taking your employees' good opinion of themselves away

Southwest Airlines has a world-class reputation for customer and employee satisfaction. One of their tactics is to "fire" the wrong customer (abusive, inebriated, or just those with an expectation that Southwest cannot exceed) while pulling out the stops for the right customer. That could never happen without a clear idea of the value of the right customer and the costs of the wrong customer.

LISTENING TO THE VOICE OF THE MARKETPLACE

Recently, we received a great compliment from a new client. The senior VP said, "I've noticed that you guys are professional listeners. Teach me how."

Most businesspeople think that listening is as easy as *not talking*. It's not. Listening takes a host of talents and more energy than delivering that big speech to shareholders.

It does no good to get close to customers if you aren't listening. In fact, it probably does more harm by spoiling illusions they might draw from your absence.

The first attribute a listener needs is empathy. Michael Eisner has written that what brings managers down isn't "the lack of understanding some arithmetic table, not the lack of understanding what the information highway is, but the lack of understanding of why somebody is unhappy." He's talking about empathy.

If your organization acts like "those customers are irrational," you're hearing that they are out of touch with the customers' rationale. Empathy informs you what it feels like to be in someone else's circumstances. It connects you with what makes them happy or unhappy.

At Cisco, CEO John Chambers grades senior VPs on how many customer calls they do each quarter and what the customer had to say about the executive's visit. And Chambers gets a nightly report of customers with network problems and the potential to be unhappy.

The second attribute of a great listener is curiosity: to be able to shelve your innate self-absorption, admit you don't have all the answers, and open up to new information.

The last attribute is patience. Great listeners are made, *not* born. It takes hundreds of sessions to figure out how to get in sync quickly, ask questions the right way, and hear what goes unsaid as well as said.

START LIKING YOUR CUSTOMERS

The head of banquet services for a major hotel chain said to us recently, "My job would be great if it weren't for the customers." He found them difficult and unappreciative. And his reaction was "Right back at you . . ." (Just imagine the things he could do to make your food and event miserable.)

Lots of executives feel the same way. If they didn't feel that way, our efforts to get top managers to spend 50 percent of their time face-to-face with actual customers with actual concerns wouldn't meet with so much resistance, whining, and excuses. As the CEO of MTV Networks said, "a young staff that genuinely *like* their customers' tastes" is the reason for his success.

The leaders of every company we studied who have demonstrated the ability to maintain velocity share something else in common: they stay close to their customers. Steve Case is an AOL customer and under several different aliases he spends hours each day using and exploring his company's service. Leo Pujals regaled in popping in unannounced and undercover to Telepizza locations simply to eat his firm's products. Charles Schwab and his company leaders are also Schwab customers. And nothing excites the leadership of H&M like spending time on their shop floors as both sellers and customers.

By contrast—and it may appear to be painting with a broad brush, but the observation is based on twenty years of working with thousands of companies—the executives at most companies sit in their spacious office suites and go to extraordinary lengths to have nothing to do with their customers. If you want your organization to stay fast, like your customers.

[A SIXTY-SECOND HEADS-UP]

- Finding, keeping, and growing the "right" customers requires knowing and liking them.
- Doing business with the wrong customers will eventually slow an organization down.
- Marginal buyers cause employee and good customer burnout.
- Every marginal deal requires the same financial resources as the best-paying customers.
- Listening to customers isn't the same as not talking.
- Listening requires empathy, curiosity, and patience.
- Be an anonymous customer of your own business to really know what it's like.

ADAPT, IMPROVISE, AND OVERCOME

*B*attlefield veterans provide companies that wish to sustain momentum a unique point of view on forecasting and planning: "No plan, however well thought out, survives contact with the enemy" (taken from a *War Manual for Tank Commanders* found on the Internet). That is, battle conditions require fast, effective responses to events as they unfold. And up against the thousands of possible moves all coming down in real time, it is incredible to expect things to go as the brass planned. In order to win battle after battle, a leader must build the capability among all troops to *adapt* to the situation as it is, *improvise* solutions that fit the goals and objectives without getting anyone's okay, and *overcome* the obstructions with determination and perseverance.

It's not just modern battlefields that are unstable, unsettled, and hazardous. Fluctuating market demands, hard-charging competitors, and new objectives from the top make everyday business like navigating a minefield. The fastest businesses have shifted their emphasis from doing more forecasting to becoming more nimble—making themselves able to generate quick assessments, land in the right direction, and build a team that constantly adapts, improvises, and overcomes.

ADAPT FAST OR PERISH

Look back at the Fortune 500 of 1970 and compare it to the list of 1998. You'll find 74 percent of the companies that were on the list *are off in less than thirty years*. This fits with another study that concluded the average life expectancy for a corporation is about three decades.

Now look at the 4,900 companies that went public between 1988 and 1998. Twenty-nine percent have ceased trading, and of those that remain, almost half trade below their offering prices. These days even failure is getting downsized.

The Columbia Broadcasting System (CBS) was a rock of stability for half a century. Then, in less than fifteen years, it went through four major ownership shifts: Loews (Laurence A. Tisch) took over in the late 1980s, then Westinghouse (Michael Jordan) in the early 1990s, a side step to Infinity (Mel Karmazin), and in 2000 Viacom (Sumner Redstone) has the keys to Black Rock. The lesson is: Adapt quickly or the market will do it for you.

But getting everyone to see the need to adapt is surprisingly difficult. Everyone nods and agrees in meetings and workshops, but when it's time to actually do it, they have a you-go-first attitude.

Over the last twenty years, we have been brought into a lot of situations where people needed to make lightning-fast adaptations.

A lot have gone well and some have not. Those that have gone well have all focused their eyes on a place the rest have avoided. They all looked deep into the jaws of hell.

PEERING INTO THE JAWS OF HELL

The jaws of hell are that body of evidence that points to your business's demise or slide into irrelevancy. It's like getting a visit from the ghost of Christmas Future where you confront facts such as:

- How underwhelming you are to your customers (in their own words) and how easily they can do without you

- How high your company's defection rate is among its best customers and employees

- How many direct and indirect competitors have pinned a bull's-eye to your back

Craig Barrett and Andy Grove once asked themselves: "What would our successors change if we were replaced by the board tomorrow?" The list they created by peering into this hellish scenario guided another in Intel's long list of successful transformations.

At Lend Lease, the company credits its success to the annual reinvention exercise created by Stuart Hornery more than two decades ago, whereby once a year everything the company does— every job, every project, every capital resource commitment—is up for discussion and grabs.

IMPROVISE

"Our hotel in Yokohama has a problem," Ichigo Umehara, president of Pan Pacific Hotels and Resorts worldwide, said to us recently at breakfast. "Our people are very professional, but they lack something."

"Like attention to every customer?" we asked. "No," he continued. "They are extremely attentive. It's just that when something comes up that is outside their normal way of dealing, they are perfunctory and almost mechanical. I would like them to be more . . . what is the word?" He paused and searched his mind for the just the right word.

"Improvisational?" we offered. "Ahh . . . exactly," said the president with a big smile. "Jamming," he nodded in agreement with his conclusion. "That is what we need them to be able to do . . . to be jamming like a jazz combo."

Jamming (or improvisation) has been defined in music as "spontaneous composition." In business, improvisation is all the efforts above and beyond the rote responses and policy book procedures used to exceed the expectations of the customer in real time. It's an on-the-spot composing of the right thing to say or do.

Thick customer manuals, annual sessions on empowerment, even that "open" letter from the chairperson urging all associates to "delight the customer," have been proven useless at improving service levels. That's because exhortations about empowerment and freedom to create are not the drivers of improvisation—developing keen instincts for employees is the driver.

TO START JAMMING, YOU NEED GOOD INSTINCTS

Intuitive decisions have a bad rep. They are seen as long on emotion and short on analysis. But gut-level instinct (or intuition) fits many of the situations we need to address in business:

- When time is of the essence

- When guidelines, policies, and rules conflict with objectives and expert guidance is unavailable

- When uncertainty prevails due to new circumstances, products, or markets

The answer is to build good instincts—those that can be consistent with your crusade and guiding principles—and to get everyone using those instincts.

In music, good improvisational instincts come by immersion, accompanying, and experimenting. That's the teaching of Marc Sabella (at www.outsideshore.com), Web author and teacher of jazz improvisation. Business can also use these principles:

IMMERSION—observation of mentors and other practitioners doing the right thing in actual situations with actual customers

ACCOMPANYING—being a part of the service process under the leadership of seasoned personnel and getting critiqued on their support

EXPERIMENTING—being given the encouragement to improvise and the freedom to be creative at the edge of the envelope.

OVERCOME

Fast businesses have come to the same conclusion: *you have to hire attitudes over skills*. Schwab, AOL, Lend Lease—all the examples in this book—have set themselves up to screen for the right attitude.

Skills can be developed, but an attitude is a deep and mysterious thing. Professionals spend years trying to undue the mess created during early life in many psyches. You just don't have the time.

When we're asked for the attitude we most want from a new hire, the answer is "proven initiative." We want to see how someone has overcome disadvantages and adversity. We want to measure resilience and ingenuity. And we favor candidates who've struggled, blown it, gotten battered or bruised, and persevered. That runs counter to the things most people look for in interviews. They look for high grades from top-notch schools, a history of success in a similar business, and all the nice things people have to say about the applicant.

To find the willingness to prevail, you have to hear about failings, weaknesses, and mistakes. A lot of success comes from luck. Until it is tested, you don't know what someone is made of. That's why boot camps and survival courses are used to train people for the most critical missions in the world.

Are you making the interview too easy and selling others on the idea of working for you rather than vice versa? Do you offer new recruits a boot camp–like environment to show them how tough things can be?

[A SIXTY-SECOND HEADS-UP] ➡

- No plan, however well thought out, survives contact with the enemy.

- Unless your company learns to adapt fast, you will perish.

- Most people should wear a T-shirt that says, "Change is great—you go first." They're lots of talk and little action.

- The fastest and most successful companies make a regular visit to the jaws of hell and peer in to see what awaits them if they are not able to change.

- Regularly ask the question à la Andy Grove: "If I was fired tomorrow, what things would my replacement do differently?" Then ... do them.

- If you want to keep moving fast, hire intuitive people who know how to jam.

*T*he two years that passed between the idea for this book and its publication have alternately been the most frustrating and exhilarating times of our professional lives. For the past twenty years, our work with thousands of companies has placed us center stage in hundreds of executive suites, boardrooms, company retreats, lecture halls, and stages. Though they've had many names, all our client assignments have essentially been the same: to help lead our clients to their full economic potential.

An observation we made years ago is as accurate today as it was when we began our practice. Most human organizations, it seems, are looking for *easy* and *effortless* answers. Most executives (including scores of high-profile managing directors and CEOs) seem to be on a constant search for sorcerers with magical answers to enter their life, wave a wand, and *poof* . . . have the job done and the pain gone. (It's even better if it doesn't require any time or effort on their part or any of their money.)

THE FRUSTRATING PART . . .

Despite years of casting one another a knowing smile, signifying we'd landed another one—another company owner or CEO looking for magical answers—we got sucked in. Once we had identified the fastest companies on the planet and asked, begged, and sometimes wiggled our way deep into these companies, we were convinced we would find magical formulas, revolutionary ideas, and life-changing methods that allowed these businesses to achieve speed, sustain momentum, and leave their competition eating dust. We were soon disappointed.

Did we unearth a few formulas to allow faster production of widgets? Sure. But not anything that wouldn't soon be available to everyone else.

Did we see some equipment that sews zippers in clothing a little faster? Yep. But we concluded that if a piece of equipment whose function could be copied by another manufacturer represented a company's sole competitive advantage, it would end up being pretty transient.

Did we uncover a few amusing tactics for keeping things moving fast—like one company's rule that all meetings are to be held with everyone standing up rather than sitting down? We did, but not enough of them to fill a book and add to a body of knowledge.

We traveled around the world many times and spent countless hundreds of hours searching for the magic formula for speed until one day the penny dropped and everything fell into place.

THE EXHILARATION . . .

As discussed earlier in the book, we concluded that speed is the natural condition. A simple reframing of our search took us on a journalistic undertaking of a lifetime. Instead of looking for magical answers as to what companies do to be fast, we began asking, "What do fast companies do to eliminate the speed bumps that slow everyone else down?"

We quickly discovered that truly fast companies that have demonstrated the ability to maintain momentum aren't naturally any faster than their slower-moving rivals. But they are smarter. Smart enough to recognize that the speed bumps that slow everyone else down must be ruthlessly eliminated, and, like killing a vampire, a stake must be driven through the heart to make certain they don't resurface.

One recurrent theme throughout this book is the need to identify and own your competitive advantage. Unless the companies profiled in this book take their eye off the ball and abandon doing the things that made them great, we have little question about their continued lightning-fast success. Each has made speed—*fast thinking, fast decisions, fast to market, and sustaining momentum*—one of their unique competitive advantages.

THE FUTURE OF SPEED

Will things become even faster? Yes. Can another financial services firm surpass Schwab's quick ascent? Will another media company move as quickly as Clear Channel in becoming the largest out-of-home media company in the world? Is it possible that another fast-food company will grow faster than Telepizza? Can another

ISP/content provider start from scratch and move as fast as AOL to the top of the heap? Will another company move faster than Hotmail? Is it likely that another fashion retailer will be able to duplicate H&M's meteoric success? The answer is a theoretical YES!

Do we think it's likely? No . . . for one simple reason . . . the human condition. Most people won't do the things they need to do—the tactics profiled in this book—to get to where they say they want to be. Eventually the speed bumps will get them.

Will other companies that today are little more than a dream in someone's mind move even faster than the ones we profiled? Yes, and when the time comes, we'd be willing to bet that an examination will reveal that these new companies achieved their speed and maintained their momentum by finding new and unique ways to blow up the speed bumps in front of them.

WE'RE NOT FINISHED WITH SPEED . . . WE'VE JUST BEGUN

During our research we not only met scores of fast people with whom we wish a continuing relationship but received hundreds of tips for future follow-up. Our work with clients has taken on new dimensions as a result of what we learned about the elimination of speed bumps.

We'll continue to study and report on speed and will regularly post our findings, publish case studies, and invite the participation of those committed to the elimination of speed bumps on our Web site itsthefast.com. From time to time, we'll even post magical answers and potions if we discover them!

It's our hope that this book will become your war manual and that it will assist you in your efforts in cracking the code of speed.

on competition, 226
on contingency plans, 48-49
on failure, 48-49, 117
fast daily response to e-mail by, 63
on fast-to-market employees, 181
guiding principles, 75, 76
on innovations, 35
and speed of e.schwab launching, 159
on storytelling to maintain momentum, 220
See also Charles Schwab
press coverage, maintaining company secrecy and, 155
principles, guiding. See guiding principles
priority setting, 203-4
Prodigy, 5, 216
profits, measuring, 207-10
project teams, 65-66
Pujals, Leopold Fernando
accomplishments, 6
as anonymous Telepizza customer, 242
on competition, 228
on fast-to-market employees, 181
idea behind Telepizza founding, 13
institutional storytelling and, 221, 222
investment growth, 202
on measuring and scoring activity, 209-10
origin of Telepizza's cause and, 126
personal background, 16, 190
personally proved operating formula, 190-193
proving the math, 47-48, 190-93
reason for founding company, 81, 190
simplicity and speed in business propositions, 167, 169
See also Telepizza

Quaker Oats, 55

radio stations, 89, 216. *See also* Clear Channel Communications
Rand McNally, 179

RCA, 216
reading, to spot trends, 33-34
reassessment, 109-20
company successes with, 110-12
four steps for, 117-20
reasons for rejecting, 112-16
Redstone, Sumner, 244
Reid, John, 174
resources, allocation of, 197-205
retreats, for annual reassessment, 119
revenue, 187-95
reversion to the means, 104-5
rewards
for big ideas, 64-65
for employees who advance crusade, 133-34
for fast-to-market employees, 184
for maintaining secrecy, 162
Richard Geist's Strategic Investments (Geist), 101
Ritter, Bruce, 101
RNZ (radio network), 89
Rohrbach, Kate, 131
Rooster.com, 156
Rules for Revolutionaries (Kawasaki), 44

Sabella, Marc, 247
sales calls, 63-64
scenario planning, 23-25
Schumpeter, Joseph, 200
Schwab, Charles
on competitive advantage of owning technology, 138, 145
disinterest in competitors, 226
guiding principles, 75, 76
and origin of company's cause, 125-26
reason for founding company, 81
reassessment and adaptability, 111
as Schwab customer, 242
and secrecy as competitive advantage, 159
See also Charles Schwab
Schwabline, 139
Scott Paper, 199
Sears, 216
secrecy, 153-63